GAMBLERS, GUNMEN, AND GOOD-TIME GALS

GAMBLERS, GUNMEN, AND GOOD-TIME GALS

Living It Up in the Wild West

HISTORY

by Valerie Green

PUBLISHED BY ALTITUDE PUBLISHING LTD.
1500 Railway Avenue, Canmore, Alberta T1W 1P6
www.altitudepublishing.com
1-800-957-6888

Extreme care has been taken to ensure that all information presented in
this book is accurate and up to date. Neither the author nor the
publisher can be held responsible for any errors.

Publisher	Stephen Hutchings
Associate Publisher	Kara Turner
Series Editor	Jill Foran
Editor	Gayl Veinotte
Digital Photo Colouring	Bryan Pezzi

We acknowledge the financial support of the Government
of Canada through the Book Publishing Industry Development
Program (BPIDP) for our publishing activities.

Altitude GreenTree Program
Altitude Publishing will plant twice as many trees as were used
in the manufacturing of this product.

Cataloging in Publication Data

Green, Valerie, 1940-
    Gamblers, gunmen and good-time gals / by Valerie Green.

(Amazing stories)
ISBN 1-55265-106-1

    1. Outlaws--Colorado--Biography. 2. Gamblers--Colorado--Biography.
3. Colorado--History--To 1876. 4. Crime--Colorado--History--19th century.
5. Colorado--Biography. I. Title. II. Series: Amazing stories (Canmore, Alta.)

F852.G78 2005   978.8'02'0922   C2005-902056-3

An application for the trademark for Amazing Stories™
has been made and the registered trademark is pending.

Printed and bound in Canada by Friesens
2 4 6 8 9 7 5 3 1

To the memory of all the legends of the Old West
and for my own little bandit, Rupert

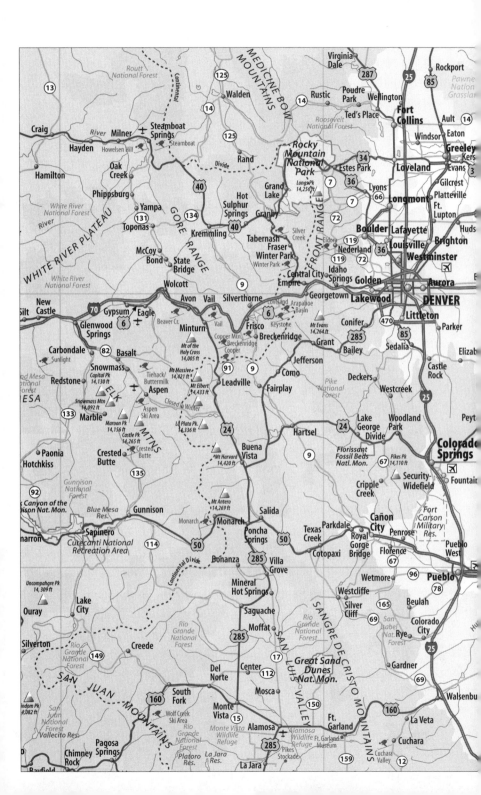

Contents

Prologue

One of Colorado's worst blizzards hit Leadville in February of 1935, keeping everyone inside or, at best, only venturing a few steps from home. By early March, it was still snowing, and the snow was more than knee deep with temperatures way below freezing.

Baby Doe lived in a run-down cabin on the outskirts of town, alongside the long silent, but once famous Matchless Silver Mine. Although an old woman now, she was still known by everyone in Leadville. On that particular day, she was one of the few to venture outside, in order to find firewood for her stove. Her shack was freezing even at the best of times, but never one to complain, she insisted on still living there. That day she decided to go down to 7th Street in search of fuel.

It was tough going, and she kept falling down. For much of the way, she crawled on her hands and knees and laughed inwardly at the picture of herself in such a ridiculous position. Her shoeless feet were wrapped in gunnysacks tied together with twine, a state of affairs poverty had forced upon her in latter years. "I still remember the satin slippers I wore so long ago," she thought to herself. "My goodness, how times have changed!" By the time she reached 7th Street, she could barely feel any of her extremities.

Gamblers, Gunmen, and Good-Time Gals

Another gentleman in town had also braved the weather that day. He saw her struggling along and immediately rushed to her aid. He helped her back to the cabin with her wood and then helped her inside. At 81 years of age, she was still well loved by many people in Leadville, despite her early scandalous life.

About a week later, a neighbor noticed there was no longer any smoke coming from the chimney of Baby Doe's cabin, and townspeople decided to send someone out to check on her. Two volunteers trudged through the snow, clearing a path as they went. They finally reached the cabin door, against which snow had drifted more than six feet high. It took a while to dig through. They knocked loudly on the door, but there was no response, so together they pushed it open.

Staring aghast, they could not believe the scene that confronted them ...

Chapter 1
The Colorado Cannibal

Already convicted of pre-meditated murder, Alfred Packer awaited sentencing on Friday, April 13, 1883. He knew that Judge Melville Gerry would not look kindly upon him and would undoubtedly condemn him to death.

Legend gives two versions of the judge's words at that final sentencing, one in the vernacular and the other in keeping with the court documents. The vernacular version carried more weight and color at the time and described the true feeling people harbored for this Colorado legend.

Supposedly, the judge said:

Stand up yah voracious man-eating sonofabitch and receive yir sintence. When yah came to Hinsdale

County, there was siven Dimmycrats. But you, yah et five of 'em, goddam yah. I sintince yah to be hanged by th' neck ontil yer dead, dead, dead, as a warnin' ag'in reducin'th' Dimmycrat populayshun of this county. Packer, you Republican cannibal, I would sintince ya to hell but the statutes forbid it.

The story began nine years earlier in mid-April of 1874, when Alfred Packer wandered alone out of the San Juan mountains and into the town of Saguache, Colorado.

He began spending money taken from several different wallets he carried on his person. Most of the money he spent in Larry Dolan's saloon, where he told anyone who cared to listen that he got lost mining in the mountains and had gone for many days without food. He did not, however, look particularly hungry and he appeared to be reasonably healthy. He also said he had injured his leg in a fall, which caused him to lag behind the others in his party. He asked around to see if any of his group had already arrived ahead of him, but no one had.

A week later he moved on to the Los Pinos Indian Agency, a short distance from Saguache, and that was when people began to get really suspicious about his behavior. He certainly did not look like a man who claimed to have been near starvation for days, and the fact that he continued to spend recklessly invited speculation about the truth of his story.

On May 1, General Charles Adams, the man in charge of the agency, returned from Denver where he had been on

Al Packer

business, and his suspicions were immediately aroused by this stranger. The next day, he and Otto Mears another agency official began to interrogate Packer to try and determine the truth.

In answer to their questions, Packer told them he was

born in Allegheny County, Pennsylvania, in November 1842, had learned how to work leather as a young man, and was soon an accomplished shoemaker. In April of 1862, when the war between the states erupted, he had enlisted in the 16th United States Infantry at Winona, Minnesota, but was honorably discharged at Fort Ontario, New York, a few months later.

"I was incapable of performing the duties of a soldier because I was diagnosed with epilepsy," he told them. He said he enlisted again in June of 1863 in the 8th Regiment of the Iowa Cavalry, but a year later was again discharged as being epileptic.

"I drifted around for many years," he continued, "but at the end of 1872, I was working in Georgetown, Colorado, as a miner's helper, and that's where I lost these two fingers on my left hand in an accident." He said he then took off for Utah, where he heard talk about the rich gold prospects back in Colorado, so he offered to act as a guide through the mountains. In late November of 1873, he led a party of 21 men eastbound from Bingham Canyon in Utah towards the San Juan Mountains in Colorado.

From then onwards, Packer's story became somewhat disjointed and it varied each time he told it. The party had obviously set off with insufficient food supply — that much was true. Then, while crossing a river by raft, they lost some of their rations. By the time they arrived at Chief Ouray's camp near Montrose in western Colorado, they were hungry and very weary. The chief offered them respite until spring when the weather would improve and they could continue their journey.

However, Packer and five other men (Shannon Wilson Bell, Israel Swan, James Humphrey, Frank "Reddy" Miller, and George "California" Noon) were all impatient to find that elusive gold, and even though they were advised by the chief that the mountain passes could be treacherous at that time of year, they ignored his advice. On February 9, they set out with a 10-day supply of food for what they thought would be a 40-mile journey. Packer claimed that the unrelenting winter weather and blinding snow had separated him from his companions. He maintained he had survived on rabbits and the occasional early rose bud bursting through the snow.

After intensive interrogation about why he had so much money on his person, Packer finally changed his story and agreed to sign the first of three confessions as to what had really occurred between February and April that year.

His confession stated:

Old man Swan died first and was eaten by the other five persons, about ten days out from camp; four or five days afterwards Humphrey died and was also eaten; he had about one hundred and thirty-three dollars and I found the pocket-book and took the money. Some time afterwards while I was carrying wood, the Butcher [Miller] was killed as the other two told me accidentally and he was eaten. Bell shot "California" with Swan's gun, and I killed Bell; shot him — covered up the remains, and took a large piece along. Then traveled fourteen days into the Agency. Bell had wanted to kill me, struck at me with his rifle, struck a tree and broke his gun.

I, A.G. Packer, do solemnly swear that the above statement is true and nothing but the truth So help me God.

In other words, Packer was maintaining that the deaths of two of the men were from exposure to the severe weather conditions and that Bell's death was in self-defense. He also confessed to cannibalism in order to survive. He had taken the money belonging to Humphrey simply because he figured Humphrey would no longer be needing it.

But something did not quite add up. Adams reported the story to Washington, but also authorized a search for the bodies in the meantime. He wanted Packer to take them back to the place where each of the five men supposedly died. Packer was then placed in the custody of Herman Lauter, the Los Pinos Indian Agency constable, and a search was carried out for several days. Packer, however, appeared to be purposely leading them down false trails. In addition, the weather did not permit a more thorough search, so in mid-May, they all returned to the agency and Adams issued a warrant for Packer's arrest for murder.

He was delivered back to Saguache, as there was no place to hold him at the agency. But it was the same situation in Saguache, so Packer was kept overnight at the home of Otto Mears and then imprisoned at a nearby ranch. On August 8, he escaped with the help of an unknown person, who obviously believed he was not guilty of murder and had only been trying to survive in unbearable circumstances.

Later that month, on August 20, John Randolph, a sketch artist for *Harper's Weekly*, was wandering through the mountains when he came upon five bodies, one of which was headless. The others had pieces of flesh torn from their bodies and had been horribly ravaged, either by man or beast. The remains lay in a group near the bank where the lake joined the Gunnison River, two miles from present-day Lake City.

Randolph began to sketch the scene and then reported his findings to the county coroner. An inquest was held, and the bodies were identified by Preston Nutter, a member of the original party of prospectors, as being the five missing members of Alfred Packer's group. They seemed to have been murdered together in their sleep, and not to have died at various times from starvation along the trail as Packer had stated. The coroner organized a mass burial on a high bluff nearby, and separate monuments were erected to each man. The area became known as "Dead Man's Gulch."

When word reached Saguache, however, Packer had already escaped and for the next few years managed to elude the law as he wandered through Arizona, Montana, and Wyoming. A warrant for his arrest was issued by the justice of the peace in San Juan City, Orlando A. Messler. Packer was now wanted "dead or alive."

However, it was not until March of 1883, some nine years later, that Packer was finally found. He had been living under the assumed name of John Schwartze while traveling, but was identified by Frenchy Cabizon, a member of the original prospecting party that had left Utah with Packer. Cabizon heard Packer's unusual laugh one day in a saloon in Fort Fetterman, Wyoming, and immediately recognized him. Cabizon reported his find to the authorities, who captured Packer and took him into custody at Wagon Hound Creek, about 30 miles west of Fort Fetterman where he had been living.

Under arrest, Packer traveled back by train to be imprisoned in Gunnison. The train stopped in Denver on March 16, 1883, and there Packer made his second confession, a slightly more detailed account of the events that happened. Again, the confession was made in front of General Adams. Newspaper reporters also hounded Packer in Denver, all eager for a story about a man accused, but not charged, of cannibalism. At that point, he had only been charged with murder.

Packer's second confession went into far more detail. He described how he and the five other men had left Chief

Ouray's Camp in February with only enough provisions for one man. After two or three days, it began to snow heavily and soon became so deep they were forced to climb higher up the mountains to a range area. By the end of the fourth day, they had approximately one pint of flour left among them.

On the 10th day out, Packer claimed they were all so hungry and exhausted that they were becoming disoriented and acting crazy. They were living on rosebuds and pine gum only, and most of the men were crying or praying. When they found a stream, they cut holes in the ice to catch fish, but there were no fish to be had, so they ate snails. By then, the men were also becoming angry, and Swan ordered Packer to go up higher in the mountains to find them something to eat. "After all, I was their leader and their guide," said Packer.

"I was gone for nearly a day, but only found one big rosebush with a few buds. Snow was everywhere in all directions. When I came back to camp, I found the redheaded man [Bell] acting crazy, sitting near the fire roasting a piece of meat which he had cut out of the leg of the German butcher [Miller]. The body was lying the furthest off from the fire down the stream, his skull was crushed in with the hatchet."

Packer then described how the bodies of the other three men were nearer the fire, all cut in the forehead with the hatchet. Bell suddenly noticed Packer approaching and raised the hatchet to attack, rushing toward the man. Packer did not hesitate, because he knew what his fate would be if Bell reached him, so he shot Bell in the stomach. Bell fell forward, the hatchet falling ahead of him. Packer grabbed it and hit Bell over the head to make sure he was dead.

That night, Packer camped by the fire, but could not sleep. He was now alone, his companions all dead, and fear was taking over all rational thought. Next day, he tried again to find a way out, first higher up the mountain and then sideways into some pine timber, where he eventually set up two sticks and covered them over with pine boughs, making a three-foot-high shelter.

"That was my camp until I came out," he said. "I went back to the fire and covered the men up and fetched to my new camp the piece of meat that was near the fire. I made a new fire near my camp and cooked the piece of meat and ate it. I tried to get away every day, but could not because of the snow, so I lived off the flesh of these men, the bigger part of the 60 days I was out."

His confession astounded his listeners, but there was more to come, and it was even worse. Apparently the weather slowly improved and Packer decided to try again to make it out of the mountains. Before he left, however, he cooked some of the flesh and carried it with him in a bag, together with one blanket, a gun, and $70 he found on the men — plus the 20 he himself had — making $90 in all.

"At my last camp before I reached the agency, I ate the last pieces of meat ... I could not eat but a little at a time."

He admitted that when he had taken the party out

to search for the bodies, he only went as far as the stream, because he could not face revisiting the camp where the atrocities had taken place.

"When I was at the Sheriff's office in Saguache," he added, "I was passed a key made out of a penknife blade with which I could unlock the irons. I then fled to Arkansas and worked all summer for John Gill, 18 miles below Pueblo, then I rented Gilbert's ranch still further down, put in a crop of corn, sold it to John Gill and went to Arizona."

This second confession of Packer's was sworn to on March 16, 1883 in the County of Arapaho, State of Colorado. Once again, Packer swore that it was true. It would not, however, be his last confession.

He was sent to Lake City at the Hinsdale District Court to be tried for the murder of Israel Swan, because, according to witnesses, Swan's remains showed evidence of a struggle, indicating there had been a violent altercation between Swan and his killer. Packer, on the other hand, had admitted only to killing Bell and that in self-defense.

The presiding judge at the April 6, 1883 trial was Judge Melville Gerry, and the first witness to be called was Preston Nutter, the man who had initially identified the five victims. For some reason, the coroner was never called to the stand.

When Packer stood to defend himself, he lied about several things, including his age, the nature of his military service, and his epilepsy. He seemed to be confused about everything, but he still denied vehemently that he had been responsible for the deaths of any of the party, other than that of Wilson Bell in self-defense. However, he still gave contradictory statements as to how and when the other deaths occurred.

By then, Packer had given several versions of his experiences in the mountains, and he had also admitted to stealing money, so things were certainly not going well for him. On the witness stand, he had appeared argumentative when cross-examined but, despite everything, he still believed the jury would look favorably upon him. They did not. He was convicted of the premeditated murder of Israel Swan and condemned to death.

Judge Gerry was a literate man and, according to the court documents of the trial, pronounced Packer's sentence in the following words:

> *Close up your ears to the blandishments of hope.*
> *Listen not to its flattering promises of life; but pre-*
> *pare for the dread certainty of death. Prepare to*
> *meet thy God; . . .*

> *Alfred Packer, the judgment of this Court is that you*
> *be removed hence to the jail of Hinsdale County,*
> *and there be confined until the 19th day of May,*
> *A.D. 1883, and that on said 19th day of May 1883,*
> *you be taken from thence by the Sheriff of Hinsdale*
> *County, to a place of execution prepared for this*

*purpose, at some point within the corporate limits
of the town of Lake City ... and between the hours
of 10 a.m. and 3 p.m. of said day, you then and
there, by the said Sheriff, be hung by the neck until
you are dead, dead, dead, and may God have mercy
upon your soul.*

Packer's fate was not yet quite sealed, however, and the verdict was appealed. Because many folk felt strongly about the horrendous crime of cannibalism, authorities feared a lynching. Packer was removed from Lake City to Gunnison as the appeal went forward, and his execution was stayed.

Two years later, Packer was re-tried in Gunnison after the Colorado Supreme Court put aside the murder conviction based on a technical oversight. It seemed that a man could not be tried in 1883 for a crime he had committed in 1874, because there had been no state murder statute in 1874 allowing for such an occurrence. Packer had been arrested for a crime when Colorado was still a territory, but he was tried after Colorado had become a state. In addition, he had committed a crime on an Indian reservation, and so should have been tried in a federal, not a state, court.

In any event, his new trial was set for July of 1896, and this time, he was tried for all five deaths on a charge of voluntary manslaughter. Once again he was found guilty, but this time sentenced to 40 years (eight for each of the five deaths) and was placed in the state penitentiary.

Packer was a model prisoner. He made and sold pocket watches to prison visitors and also cultivated flowers in a plot of ground that was allocated to him by the warden. Through the years, attorneys began to take a renewed interest in his case and applied for retrials and even pardons.

Meanwhile, on August 7, 1897, Packer himself wrote a letter to D. C. Hatch of the *Denver Rocky Mountain News*, in which he included a third confession, the longest to date, setting out details of events that occurred on that mountain pass back in 1874.

He wrote about a man named Lutzenheiser who, with four other men, had set out before him from Chief Ouray's camp, having been told that the agency was only 40 miles away when it was really 80. They also ran out of supplies and were near starvation. That party was fortunately found, and Packer claimed that those events were all on record.

He then claimed that he and his party set out a week after Lutzenheiser with provisions that lasted only about nine days. As hunger set in, they even cooked and ate their rawhide moccasins and then wrapped their feet in blankets.

"Our suffering at this time was most intense," Packer wrote. "Such, in fact, that the inexperienced cannot imagine."

He repeated his story about returning to the camp to find Bell with the "look of a terrible maniac, his eyes glaring and burning fearfully, and he grabbed a hatchet and started for me, whereupon I raised my Winchester and shot him."

He discovered all the others dead, obviously at the

hand of Bell. He wrote "Can you imagine my situation — my companions dead and I left alone, surrounded by the midnight horrors of starvation, as well as those of utter isolation? My body weak, my mind acted upon in such an awful manner that the greatest wonder is that I ever returned to a rational condition."

He stated that for days his mind wandered, and he recalled that the first time he was forced to "take a piece of the flesh and boil it to eat it," he was sick and suffered most terribly. He added, "My mind at this period failed me."

His letter was completely repentant, penned by a man who wished "in this darkest hour of earthly existence that I would have been far better off had my execution taken place years ago, and I might now be with those companions, whose ghosts, I assure you do not haunt me [because] each and every one of those unfortunate men knows that I am innocent." He insisted that no human being could say that he had killed in cold blood with evil intent, because there would have been no point.

"No man can be more heartily sorry for the acts of twenty-four years ago than I. I am more a victim of circumstances than of atrocious designs."

His letter touched the hearts of many, and in early January of 1900, reporter Polly Pry of the *Denver Post* began to investigate Packer's case and write about him. She strongly believed in Packer's innocence and began a campaign for his release. Her endeavors reached the ears of the governor and when Packer put in another plea for parole, Governor Charles Thomas granted it to him as his last official act. It was, however, a conditional parole, which confined Packer to the State of Colorado.

Polly Pry and lawyer William Anderson had definitely been the ones who had assisted Packer in being granted parole, but it was soon discovered that Bonfils and Tammen, the owners of the *Denver Post* had really wanted Packer released so that they could put him in the Sells-Floto Circus as a sideshow man-eating freak. The governor discovered this, and so to spare Packer that humiliation, he made Packer sign a parole agreement that stated, "he should proceed to Denver and there remain, if practicable, for a period of at least six years and nine months from that date." He would not, therefore, be able to join the circus.

While he had been a prisoner over the previous 16 years, Packer had earned about $1,500 making hair rope and hair bridles, so he was able to pay his lawyer's fee of $25. The *Denver Post* owners demanded half the fee, and an argument developed in Bonfils's office between Bonfils, Tammen, Polly Pry, and Anderson. Bonfils struck Anderson in the face, so Anderson went across the street, got his gun, and returned to the office. Without knocking, he walked in and shot Bonfils in the neck and chest, and Tammen in the shoulder and chest. Both men ducked under Polly's full skirt. Anderson only had one bullet left, having shot four times, but suddenly the whole situation struck him as funny. Bonfils and Tammen were shaking and hiding under a woman's skirt. Anderson started to laugh, even when he was arrested for the crime of assault with intent to murder. He was tried three times and finally found not guilty. The trial judge told Anderson: "Your motive was admirable, but your marksmanship was abominable."

Meanwhile, Alfred Packer spent his final days in Deer Creek, managing two mines and living on his $25 a month military disability pension, which he received due to his supposed epilepsy. He always enjoyed the company of children and frequently told them the stories of his adventures in the mountains. He did, however, suffer from liver and stomach ailments, and on April 23, 1907, died of a stroke brought about, it was stated, from "senility, troubles, and worry." He was buried in Littleton, Colorado, at the government's expense. The government also provided a tombstone that read: "Alfred Packer, Co.F, 16 U.S. Inf. in recognition of his military service."

This, however, was not the end of the Alfred Packer story. No one ever forgot him in Colorado, and discussions about whether he was innocent or guilty continued for decades. Then, in 1989, James Starrs, a law professor from George Washington University in Washington, D.C., visited Gunnison. He had always been interested in the Packer trials, confessions, and defense, and was curious about the place where the victims had been buried in Dead Man's Gulch. A monument had been erected there, and Starrs decided to ask for permission to do an archeological dig, which he wrote about in the newsletter *Scientific Sleuthing Review.*

The dig began on July 17, 1989, and involved anthropologists, archeologists, photographers, students, and forensic personnel. After careful examination, the remains of five bodies were discovered side by side and were taken to a lab at the University of Arizona. Using modern-day techniques, they examined the bones and made some conclusive observations, including the fact that nicks on the bones indicated a knife had been used for de-fleshing.

Although Starrs stated that, in his opinion, Packer was indeed a murdering cannibal and liar, not everyone on his team agreed. Indeed, it would seem that Starrs's results could also prove that Packer's story had been true, if Bell had been the one to kill the other four and then was shot by Packer.

In 1998, a curator at the Museum of Western Colorado in Gunnison claimed to have Packer's actual revolver — an 1862 Colt taken from the massacre site at the time the bodies were initially discovered. At that time, there were three bullets in the chamber, and this would agree with at least one of Packer's confessions. Even if Packer had owned that gun, however, it would still not prove he had killed in self-defense, because he might have used up two other bullets to kill game or he might have murdered any of the other five.

So, the guilt or innocence of Alfred Packer, the Colorado cannibal, remains unsolved. Tourists still flock to his grave site every year and ponder the case: was he indeed a vicious murderer and cannibal or was he merely the victim of an unbelievable horror so many years ago?

Chapter 2
King of the Con Men

The young boy mingled with the crowd on one of Abilene's busiest street corners. He soon became fascinated by a man doing amazing things with three walnut shells on a table. The man's fast-moving hands were twisting the shells back and forth across the table. He had placed a pea under one of them. Each time he stopped, someone in the crowd placed a bet as to which shell contained the pea. It was always the wrong shell.

The boy, whose name was Jefferson Randolph Smith, realized that the man was a con artist. He knew that there must be a trick to his game but he, like the rest of the gullible crowd, had been taken in by the trickery each time and had, in fact, used up all his hard-earned money trying to outfox the fox himself. He never did, of course, and as with the others who hoped they would win, Smith always lost.

In fact, 16-year-old Smith lost all his money that day, and it was a hard lesson for him to learn. He had spent the last four months on a cattle drive bringing cattle into Abilene and had made a great deal of money in the process. Now it was all gone. If the experience had taught him anything at all, it was that if he had been as smart as that con artist, he would have earned twice as much money in one week than he had driving cattle in the hot sun eight hours every day for four months. That night, he made a decision. He vowed he would learn the trade himself and become a professional gambler and con artist. It was a decision he would never regret.

Smith was born in Georgia in 1860 into a wealthy southern family that, like many others, was destroyed financially by the Civil War. The family then moved to Texas to begin a new life, and Smith was given a good education, as befit his father's position as a lawyer of note. He soon became an eloquent speaker who could quote the scriptures and most of the classics, but his education did little good when it came to finding a job. At 16 he left home to sign on with a cattle drive heading to Abilene, Kansas. And it was there that he found his calling in life as a gambler and con artist.

For the next 10 years, Jefferson Smith roamed the frontier, mixing with outlaws as well as gamblers, and often ending up on the wrong side of the law. It was gambling that really excited him, though, and he was determined to

Jefferson Randolph "Soapy" Smith

become the best poker player in the west. Smith arrived in Leadville, Colorado, in 1885. The streets were packed with people trying to make a fast buck. One of the first people he met there was a man known simply as Old Man Taylor. Smith had heard a lot about him when he was still a boy back in Texas. Taylor was reputedly the "King of the Shell Game." Smith asked him if he could be his partner. He figured that with Taylor's skills and his own (which had also improved considerably by then) plus his gift of the gab, the two of them could make a lot of money.

Taylor agreed, and before too long, wherever they set up their "tripe" and "keister" (names used for a tripod and suitcase), the crowds flocked around to see the latest game. Once Taylor showed Smith the famous "soap trick," there was no stopping them. The game went as follows: several cakes of soap in bright blue wrapping paper were piled on a table. Smith then began his quick banter, which always attracted a large crowd:

"Cleanliness is next to godliness, friends," he would begin, "so step right up and watch me very carefully. If you want to take a chance on winning one of these little green bills wrapped inside the soap, I'll sell you that chance for the ridiculously low price of only $5."

He had twisted some $10, $20, and even $100 bills around some bars of soap and mixed them in with the others on the table. His partner, who was already mingling with the crowd, would be the first to pay $5 and pick out a bar of soap.

It would always be one that held a $100 bill, which he held up to show the amazed crowd. Of course, Smith had already primed him to know which one contained the money. The stampede was on, and soon everyone was throwing $5 bills at Smith to buy a chance at finding others with money inside.

Jefferson Smith was nimble-fingered, as well as a fast talker, so very few people ever got more than a five-cent bar of soap for their trouble. By the time Smith and Taylor folded up the table and the game was over, they had managed to fleece the crowd of hundreds of dollars.

The amazing part of it all was that often, after he had conned a number of people out of their money, he turned around and spent the money building churches, helping the poor and the widows in town, and paying for the funerals of the girls from the red-light district, who would not otherwise be buried in sacred ground. He also made it his business not to take money from the locals, but to try and fleece only the tourists who came into town. For this reason, he set up his act near Union Railway Station, so that he could greet new people when they first came off the train. Smith became a strange mix of unscrupulous scamp and honest do-gooder.

From Leadville, Smith moved on alone to Denver, where he improved his act considerably by adding entertainment. He sang and told jokes to amuse the crowd while setting up his bars of soap. On one occasion, a complaint for misrepresentation was filed against him, and he was arrested. The arresting officer could not remember his name at first, but knew that his game was "soap" so entered him in the log book as "Soapy Smith." It is believed that that was the first time the nickname was actually used formally, and from then on, it stuck. The charge was later dropped, and Soapy was released.

Soapy soon became the most successful gambler in the west and eventually opened the Tivoli Saloon and Gambling Hall in Denver. Above the door he had the words *Caveat Emptor* inscribed — Latin for Let the Buyer Beware. Luckily for Soapy, no one in Denver understood Latin!

In addition, Soapy initiated strong ties with law enforcement, so when any members of his gang of employees were arrested, Soapy was immediately informed and was able to arrange for their release. It was a good arrangement because, in return, Soapy helped the law by handing out free turkeys at Thanksgiving to the poor who would otherwise have been forced to steal them. He also donated to the church and allowed ministers to hold their services in his saloons.

Soapy even became something of a hero in Denver over an incident concerning the Glasson Detective Agency. Detectives had tried to force a confession from a pretty, young girl while holding her in their office. Soapy and friends raided the office with pistols and made them release the innocent girl. He became a hero overnight.

In 1892, Soapy heard about the silver boom happening in Creede, so he decided to move his operation there. Creede was just the sort of raw town for which Soapy had been searching. Situated as it was near the head of the Rio Grande River, which flows through the San Juan Mountains, the San Luis Valley towards Texas, and eventually to the Gulf of Mexico, Creede was the last of the silver boom towns in Colorado.

At its height, it is believed there were 10,000 people in the area of Creede alone. Originally named for Nicholas C. Creede who discovered the Holy Moses Mine, the town attracted thousands of miners, who were soon working the mines. The mines produced over $1 million worth of silver every month, and the town grew at an unbelievable rate. Money circulated in a wild frenzy, with no one there to organize things into some semblance of order.

Strolling through town, in and out of the saloons and dance halls with his gang, Soapy soon decided he could make a difference in the town and be in charge of everything that went on — if he played his cards right. His reputation had preceded him, and soon everyone wanted to be his friend, especially the gambling crowd. It did not take Soapy long to establish himself and take over all the gambling operations in Creede, but first he had to overcome one obstacle.

A certain individual by the name of Bob Ford, infamous as the man who had killed Jesse James, already thought of himself as the owner and head honcho of Creede. He was incensed by the brazen attitude of this newcomer, but Soapy had already been working all angles to ensure his own power base would be stable. He made important friends in town and accumulated a large bank roll, using his popular act and charismatic manner.

When the opportunity arose, he simply announced that he was going to run Creede and that everyone had better report to him or else. A friend of Soapy's, who had also known Bob Ford many years earlier, figured blood would be shed unless the two men soon got together and talked civilly about their differences. Ford realized that unless he co-operated with this stranger, who was far more polished and quicker-witted than he, he would probably come out the loser and be forced to leave town. He reluctantly agreed to meet with Soapy Smith. The meeting was set up and, with the help of the mediator, Soapy and Bob Ford came up with a compromise. They simply agreed to stay out of each other's way and operate in their own areas of town. But it was an uneasy peace.

Meanwhile, Soapy and his lifelong friend Joe Simmons built the New Orleans Club on Creede Avenue, and from his office above the club, Soapy organized the beginnings of a government, which provided some kind of peace and protection for the citizens of Creede. Soapy's organization soon held total power in Creede and gave aid to all those who arrived in town for honest, legitimate reasons. Those who posed a threat were promptly sent on their way. In fact, any newcomer to town was strongly advised to see Soapy first before doing anything else because, they were told, "What Soapy Smith says in this town goes!" Most people soon realized they would be a whole lot safer if they were seen to be a friend of Soapy Smith. Overnight, he had become the new dictator in town.

Despite his overpowering rule, Soapy Smith still maintained a softer image on occasion. When a visiting preacher to town was robbed of his entire collection plus his trousers one night, Soapy immediately rounded up the townsfolk and collected $600 from them so that the man could be repaid and continue with his plans to build a church in Creede.

Eventually, people grew tired of Soapy's dictatorial rule. Once he realized the way the wind was blowing, he made the decision to move on yet again and this time headed back to Denver, where he opened up a railroad ticket office. Again his operation was not totally legitimate. He advertised tickets to Chicago for $5, but when buyers arrived they were told that tickets were only sold at that price on certain days of the week and this was not one of them. Meanwhile, Soapy said, they were welcome to spend time gambling in his back room.

Just about that time, Colorado governor Davis H. Waite, decided he had had enough of Denver's lawlessness. He wanted to clean up the town and turn it into a place full of law-abiding citizens, so he called in the state militia. Soapy Smith, now going by the name of "Colonel" Smith, raised an army to fend off the state militia from city hall. There in the cupola, he took up his position with a dynamite bomb. He threatened to ignite the bomb if the militia fired at him.

It was estimated that 20,000 people turned out to watch the short-lived Battle of Denver, but soon federal troops from Fort Logan arrived to act as peacekeepers. Governor Waite finally agreed to withdraw his militia in favor of the federal soldiers and to allow the Colorado Supreme Court to settle the situation. Although Governor Waite was blamed for bringing in the militia too quickly, he was allowed to remove the commissioners and replace them with new ones. Their first act was to run Soapy Smith out of town.

After that incident, Soapy Smith wandered around the west for a while and eventually headed down to Mexico. Ever the con man, he was soon involved in yet another scam, this time with the Mexican president himself, Porfirio Diaz. Soapy tried to convince the president that Mexico needed a foreign legion and before long he had a recruiting office set up with himself acting as the enrolling officer — for a price. His game was discovered in time, and the deal fell through.

By then it was 1897, and news was reaching the Gold Rush states. Soapy was excited by another boomtown coming into existence, so he hit the trail once again and headed for Skagway, Alaska, to investigate the possibilities. He arrived in the summer of that year and soon built a saloon/casino called Jeff's Place. He also hired a gang of "helpers." He called them his "lambs," and their protection helped him run the casino in such a way that very few gamblers ever left with more money than they brought in. The ones that did leave with winnings were usually apprehended in a back alley by one of Soapy's "lambs," who stole the winnings and returned them to Soapy. Soapy then used this money to build Skagway's first telegraph station. He ran the station himself, but what the customers never knew was that the telegraph wires only extended a few hundred feet into Skagway's harbor. Oddly enough, replies to telegraphs were received (courtesy of Soapy) and often asked the men to send money back home, which Soapy's telegraph office was only too happy to arrange for the unsuspecting victim. It was the perfect scam.

Once again, Soapy was running a town, but the residents of Skagway were growing tired of him. They arranged for a group of men to run Soapy and his "lambs" out of town, but once again Soapy managed to persuade over 300 residents to form a committee for "permanent law and order," naming himself as their chairman. He even arranged the Fourth of July Parade, riding at the head as the grand marshal. People were reluctant to stop him, for many charities and groups had become benefactors of his generosity.

Then on July 7, a miner came into town with $3,000 in gold, which he stored in a hotel safe. He was soon persuaded by Soapy's "lambs" to move it to Soapy's safe, which, he was told, would be even safer than a bank. Needless to say, the gold mysteriously disappeared. The miner was incensed and starting yelling for vigilante action in order to get back his gold.

A crowd outside Soapy's saloon had organized themselves into a vigilante group, known as the Committee of

Soapy Smith's saloon in Skagway, Alaska, 1898.

101, and they told Soapy, in no uncertain terms, that he must return the gold by the next afternoon. Soapy claimed he had won it in a fair casino game and refused their request. The vigilantes held a meeting by the docks on the night of July 8, to decide their next move. But Soapy heard about it and headed down there with a group of armed men. He carried two revolvers and a double-barreled rifle and by-passed four guards, who were all unarmed. He was stopped by a man called Frank Reid, a civil engineer, who held a small pistol in his hand. Soapy already held a personal grudge against Reid (some thought over a woman) so he immediately tried to strike Reid with his rifle butt. Reid fired his pistol, but missed Soapy on the first shot. A struggle ensued and then both men fired simultaneously and fell to the ground.

Soapy Smith died immediately, and his killer lay dying with a wound to the groin. Soapy's "lambs" dispersed in all directions. Reid lingered for 12 days before going to meet his Maker, and he was buried in Skagway's cemetery with a headstone that reads, "He gave his life for the Honor of Skagway." Nearby is the headstone of an unknown prostitute that reads, "She gave her Honor for the life of Skagway."

Soapy was buried on the outskirts of the cemetery in a shallow grave, unmarked for years. Today, a plain marker states his name and dates of birth and death. He was barely 38 years old, but during his lifetime had made his mark across a continent from the southern states of America to the most northern state. Jefferson Randolph "Soapy" Smith, master con-artist and gambler extraordinaire, left behind an estate totaling a mere $250.

Chapter 3
Baby Doe —
The Silver Queen

The miners standing around the Fourth of July Mine outside Central City, Colorado, that day were astounded. Never before had they seen a woman about to work in one of the shafts — wearing men's clothing to boot! It was unheard of, and they were shocked to the core. In fact, the entire town of Central City, being somewhat strait-laced at that time, was amazed at this young woman's bravado. They were soon to learn that the wife of Harvey Doe, whose father owned the mine, was prepared to do anything. Her daring knew no limits.

She was born in Oshkosh, Wisconsin, in 1854, to wealthy Catholic parents and named Elizabeth Bonduel McCourt. Adored by all who knew her, by the time she had reached her teens, her incredible beauty caused young men to flock around her in droves, and she became known as "the Belle of Oshkosh."

Her many admirers even wrote poetry about her, praising her blond curls, her blue eyes, and her petal-soft complexion. Added to her dazzling beauty was a sharp wit and a charming personality that endeared her to everyone. Early on in life, Elizabeth had also displayed an independent nature and a determination to become something special. Unlike her five siblings, who preferred anonymity, Elizabeth was cursed with an adventurous spirit that drove her throughout her long life.

The combination of Elizabeth's vivacious Irish personality and her innocent, cherub-like expression brought her much attention, especially in the winter of 1876 when she entered and won the Oshkosh Congregational Church figure skating contest. This was an unheard of accomplishment for a woman at that time, but the event and the publicity surrounding it caused her to be noticed by a young man named Harvey Doe, Jr., who, like many others before him, fell madly in love with her.

This time, Elizabeth was also smitten, and the young couple married soon after and immediately boarded a train for Denver. From there they went on to Central City, Colorado, where Harvey's father owned a half-interest in a mine which he hoped his son would work and make profitable.

"We'll go west and make our fortune overnight," Harvey told his new bride. "People do it all the time out there!" And

Elizabeth's adventurous spirit believed him. Unfortunately, she soon discovered her new husband was lazy, and much preferred to drink and gamble all day rather than work. That was when she realized that if they were to become rich, it would be up to her; so she donned her husband's mining clothes and went to work in his place.

After their initial shock, the miners soon realized that this was no ordinary woman. Lizzie, as they first called her, was full of spunk and worked just as hard as any man. They began to hold her in high regard and gave her the nickname that would stick with her for the rest of her life — "Baby" Doe. She became the miners' sweetheart.

As Harvey Doe drifted from one job to the next and sometimes from one town to another, always searching for something he could never find, Baby realized she no longer wanted to be the wife of a man with little or no ambition. Harvey was by then heavily in debt, and their Fourth of July Mine was paying less than they had hoped. Despite several attempts at reconciliation in their floundering marriage, they finally divorced in 1878. The following year, Baby visited Leadville. She really liked this town and decided to move there permanently in 1881, a move that was to seal her fate and her destiny.

While dining at Leadville's elegant Saddle Rock Restaurant on that first visit, Baby Doe had attracted the attention of a very wealthy and prominent citizen, Horace Tabor. When Tabor spotted her across the room, he thought she was the most exquisite creature he had even seen.

Tabor had come to that area in 1860 with his wife, Augusta, and their son, Maxcy, having left behind a farm in Kansas. They headed first for Denver, where they heard about the mining successes in the California Gulch area, south of present-day Leadville. Augusta was a hard-working woman, but she was also often dour and moody. Nonetheless, she stuck by her husband; when the Gulch area was all panned out by 1862, the Tabors headed to Buckskin Joe. There they built a cabin, and for nearly 17 years Augusta supported her husband's attempts to make a living as he prospected the area, ran a small store selling supplies to the miners, acted as postmaster, and sat on the school board. Augusta also cooked for the miners and took in boarders, but the harsh life in a wild, frontier town aged her far too quickly. Eventually, the Tabors returned to the California Gulch and opened up another store. When they moved to Leadville itself, Tabor became the city's first mayor and its second postmaster.

All that changed overnight in 1877, when two German immigrant prospectors, August Rische and George Hook, asked Tabor to grubstake them. Tabor agreed, and the first payment to them cost him a mere $17. Within a month, they had hit the bonanza at the Little Pittsburgh Mine and by summer's end were able to declare a dividend of $10,000 to each of the partners. The silver vein strike was the biggest in Leadville's history, and Tabor became a millionaire. He continued to buy up more mines with his profits, including the famous Matchless Mine, and soon became the accepted leader of the silver mining community. His political aspirations also eventually led him to become a lieutenant-governor of Colorado.

Tabor enjoyed his new life as a wealthy man and spent his money on elaborate clothes, jewelry, and on the building of the Tabor Opera House in town. Augusta was more cautious with her money and did not enjoy her husband's frivolous new lifestyle. When he also became attracted to a beautiful 25-year-old blond, so many years his junior, she became bitter and heartbroken.

Baby Doe also fell in love with Horace Tabor, but she wanted their relationship to be discreet. She knew he was a married man, so she insisted their affair be carried on in secret, first at the Clarendon Hotel in Leadville and later at the elegant Windsor Hotel in Denver; both accommodations were paid for by Tabor. Despite being discreet, their affair was soon discovered, and Baby Doe was referred to as the notorious "other woman."

By July of 1880, Tabor was desperate to be free of his wife. He was madly in love for the first time in his life and he wanted to marry his paramour, so he asked Augusta for a divorce. At first, she refused. This led Tabor to consult with lawyers in order to secure a divorce without her permission. The divorce, granted to him in Durango, Colorado, was not totally legal, but Tabor still went ahead and secretly married his beloved Baby Doe in St. Louis on September 20, 1882.

When Augusta got wind of the bogus divorce and Tabor's remarriage, she was furious and tried to contest it.

She continued to fight vigorously for her rights, claiming that her husband was worth more than $9 million and that he should offer her a substantial sum of money. She also wanted him to maintain her for the rest of her life. After a while, she grew tired of fighting, so, still suffering from a broken heart, poor Augusta settled for $300,000 and left Leadville to settle in California. She most probably was entitled to a whole lot more considering that Horace Tabor was making approximately a million dollars a year. But Augusta could not bear to stay in Colorado as the discarded wife, while her rich husband flaunted his young lover, and his own fame grew. Augusta died a few years later, on February 1, 1895, many claimed from a broken heart.

Despite the scandal his divorce and affair had caused in political circles, Tabor still managed to secure a 30-day appointment in Henry Teller's vacated senatorial position and was sworn in as a senator on February 3, 1883. His lifestyle with Baby Doe was still front-page news in Washington and was becoming something of an embarrassment. Once Tabor's divorce from Augusta was finally legalized, he married Baby Doe the following month in a second ceremony, this time in a lavish and very public way in Washington. Even the president himself was invited. Tabor and Baby Doe wanted the whole world to know they were finally joined in a legitimate ceremony and were truly man and wife.

Baby Doe — The Silver Queen

The elite of Capitol Hill in Washington still circulated rumors about Baby Doe's so-called "shameless past." She was a divorced woman who had snared a rich, older man. They believed she was only after his money and sympathized with his discarded wife.

Once back in Denver, Baby and Tabor settled happily into their rich lifestyle. Baby shared her husband's dream of turning Denver into "the Paris of the West." It was a grand adventure for the young woman from Oshkosh, and she relished the whirlwind of champagne breakfasts, parties, travel, and political campaigns, while her husband purchased even more mines, which yielded millions of dollars worth of silver. The couple enjoyed spending evenings at the Tabor Grand Opera House and entertaining in their large Denver mansion, which had over 100 peacocks on the lawn. Tabor draped his young wife in jewelry, furs, and beautiful gowns — the latest fashion from Paris. In spite of it all, Baby never quite fit in with Denver's elite high society. The wives of Denver's richest men still considered her an upstart and thought she and her husband were socially improper, he being 26 years her senior. To them, she would always be the brazen young hussy who had pursued a married man and stolen him from his wife.

Nonetheless, the Tabors were ecstatically happy and shared a loving marriage for many years. They were also blessed with two daughters, Elizabeth (Lilly) and Rose Mary (Silver Dollar). Tragically, their only son was stillborn. There was also an unsubstantiated report that Baby Doe had, much

earlier, had another stillborn son while married to Harvey
Doe. At the time, it had been rumored that the baby was
probably not Harvey's and that her pregnancy was a result
of a liaison with one Jake (Sands) Sandelowsky, a handsome,
dark, curly-haired clothing merchant who had befriended
her in Central City when Harvey was away on his many trips.
It was true that Baby and Jake were often seen together at
the Shoo-Fly Saloon, but she considered him her friend and
supporter rather than her lover. The fact that Harvey Doe
was a regular frequenter of brothels and had been unfaithful
to his wife on numerous occasions mattered little in the eyes
of those who judged only women's behavior, which was supposed to be beyond reproach. A love affair with Jake Sands
was never proven, but the rumors added to Baby Doe's so-
called scandalous past. In her journal for the year 1879 there
is, however, a notation describing the baby she had given
birth to that year. She wrote: "My baby boy born July 13, 1879,
had dark, dark hair, very curly, and large blue eyes. He was
lovely." She might well have been describing Jake Sands.

In 1893, the fairy tale existence of Horace and Baby Tabor
suddenly turned into a nightmare. Horace Tabor had made
the mistake of putting all his eggs in one silver basket. He did
not believe in diversification and, therefore, all his wealth was
tied up in silver mining interests. The United States Treasury
decided to lower the value of silver. Within days, all Tabor's
holdings were worthless. In addition, he had made some
unwise investments in foreign mining ventures and lost large

amounts of money in Mexico and South America. The Silver King and Queen of Denver were no more.

The Tabors moved out of their mansion into a rented cottage, and those people who had always disliked Baby predicted that she would now leave her husband because he had lost all his money. They assumed she would search for another millionaire to take his place, because she was still young and very beautiful. They could not have been more wrong.

Baby stuck by her husband and remained optimistic, declaring that one day they would regain their fortune. She stayed loyal to Tabor, and their loving marriage continued to be strong through the hard times. Horace Tabor kept working at anything he could find and, at 65 years of age, he was seen shoveling slag at the Cripple Creek mines for $3 a day. One year before his death, he was appointed postmaster of Denver. He eventually died in the spring of 1899 from appendicitis. Flags were lowered to half-mast in Leadville at the news of Horace Tabor's death, and it was said that over 10,000 people attended his funeral.

Shortly before his death, Tabor had supposedly told Baby to "hang on to the Matchless" — the mine they both believed would one day revive and prosper. For the next 36 years, Baby followed his wishes to the letter, almost to the point of paranoia. She did everything in her power to try and raise money in order to work the mine once more. But the mine always proved worthless, and Baby Doe Tabor continued to live in poverty.

She moved into a run-down cabin alongside the mine and began making notes, most of which were mere ramblings, about how her fortunes would one day be reversed. As her daughters grew to adulthood, they both deserted her, tired of her single-mindedness to a worthless cause. Leadville's era of greatness had long since passed, but Baby Doe Tabor refused to accept the inevitable.

She became a legend in Leadville, living the life of a pauper in her cabin alongside a defunct silver mine. Two books were written about her and a Hollywood movie was made, telling the story of the great love affair she had shared with Horace Tabor. Countless articles, two operas, and a stage play were also written about the once wealthy Silver Queen. In 1982, Evelyn Furman, then the owner of the Tabor Opera House, wrote a book about the tempestuous life of "Silver Dollar" Tabor, Baby's daughter, in which Silver Dollar describes herself as "a leaf in the storm."

But nothing could compare with the last days of Baby Doe Tabor's life. By then it was March of 1935, and Leadville was experiencing one of its worst winters to date. Baby Doe was still living in the small cabin beside the Matchless Mine, courtesy of the current owners. Her family had deserted her. At 81, she was completely alone and reduced to extreme poverty.

It continued to snow for days and Baby soon ran out of wood for her stove. She might well have remembered a remark her husband had once made to her long ago.

"You're always so gay, Baby, and always laughing, and yet you're so brave, too. Augusta is a damned brave woman too, but she's powerful disagreeable about it."

Well, thought Baby, now was one more time for her to laugh and be brave, so she decided to set off through the snow to 7th Street in order to find wood for her stove. Her feet were covered in gunny sacking, and this amused her too, as she thought about the silver slippers she had once worn. A howling wind and a below zero temperature greeted her as she opened the cabin door, but it did not deter her. She smiled to herself as she kept falling in the snow and was grateful when a neighbor, a Mr. Zaitz, assisted her on the way home, helping to carry her wood and then opening her cabin door to help her inside.

"God bless you," she said as she sank into a chair. "I'll be fine now." He smiled warmly at Colorado's legend as he closed the door behind him. All the way home he thought about her, so poor now when once she had been so wealthy. Those wondrous years were now gone for Baby Doe. "Riches to rags," he muttered to himself as he shook his head in bewilderment at the twists and turns of fate.

Baby Doe was alone again, but she managed to start up a fire, and soon the cabin had a modicum of warmth once more. She kept the fire going for a few more days as she continued her now delirious writings in her journal.

Her neighbors, none of whom was venturing outside in the fierce blizzard, which continued to rage, were content in the knowledge that Baby Doe must be all right, because smoke continued to waft from her chimney. When it stopped, they became concerned and decided to send out a search party to check on her.

Two neighbors dug a path through the snow towards her cabin. It was hard going, as the snow was well over six feet deep in places by then. They reached her door, also piled high with a snowdrift. It took a while to burrow through and push open the door, and all the while they called out to Baby Doe Tabor, but there was no answer.

They stood for a moment in shock at the sight that greeted them inside the cold cabin. Baby Doe lay frozen on the floor, her arms peacefully crossed over her chest, her journal beside her. The Silver Queen was dead. They removed their hats and bowed their heads in respect. Baby Doe Tabor's body was sent to Denver to be buried beside her beloved Horace in Mount Olivet Cemetery.

News of her death quickly spread, as did the fact that 17 iron trunks belonging to her were known to have been placed in storage in Denver, together with gunny sacks full of her belongings. When the trunks and gunny sacks were opened, they were found to contain a number of bolts of very expensive, exotic silk cloth, pieces of exquisite china, a tea service, and some jewelry, which included a diamond and sapphire ring. There was also the pocket watch and fob, which had been presented to Horace Tabor at the grand opening of the $700,000 Tabor Opera House in Denver.

Any one of those items could have been sold off by Baby during her last 36 years on earth, and their worth would have enabled her to live a more comfortable life. Instead, she had chosen to live out the rest of her life alongside a worthless silver mine, dreaming a dream that never materialized.

Chapter 4
The Gambling Dentist

No one knew Doc Holliday better than Wyatt Earp. Their friendship and affection for one another lasted for many years. Earp once summed up his feelings for Holliday in the following words:

I found him to be a loyal friend and good company. He was a dentist whom necessity had made a gambler; a gentleman whom disease had made a vagabond; a philosopher whom life had made a caustic wit; a long, lean, blonde fellow nearly dead with consumption and at the same time the most skilful gambler and nerviest, speediest, deadliest man with a six-gun I ever knew.

Holliday had traveled a long and varied road prior to meeting Wyatt Earp and taking part in the famous Gunfight at the OK Corral, which made his name renowned in the history of the old west. He spent much of his time in Colorado and was involved in many encounters on both sides of the law.

He was born in Griffin, Georgia, in August 1851, to Henry and Alice Holliday, well-to-do southerners. The year before John Henry's birth, the Hollidays had lost their first-born child — a six-month-old daughter, Martha Eleanora — and so were very happy to now have a healthy son. The family moved to Valdosta in 1857, where Henry Holliday had inherited some land. He was a pharmacist by profession and later became a lawyer and then, in Valdosta, a plantation owner, making a great deal of money along the way. During the Civil War, he rose to the rank of Confederate major.

In September 1866, when young John Henry was only 15 years old, his mother died from consumption, an event that was to affect his whole life. He had been very close to his mother and loved her dearly, so her death caused him considerable sorrow. Then three months later, his father re-married. This compounded John's grief.

Major Holliday had by then become a leading citizen in Valdosta. He served as mayor and as secretary of the County Agricultural Society, as well as joining the Masonic Lodge and acting as secretary of the Confederate Veterans Camp and superintendent of local elections. He gave his son a good education and helped to steer him into a reputable profession by enrolling him in dental school in 1870. John attended lecture sessions between 1870 and 1872 and wrote his thesis entitled, *Diseases of the Teeth.* He also served his required two years' apprenticeship under Dr. L. Frank.

In March of 1872, John Henry Holliday received his degree from the Pennsylvania College of Dental Surgery in Philadelphia and became a doctor of dental surgery. He was ready to open his first office and did so in partnership with Dr. Arthur Ford in Atlanta later that same year.

Soon after he began his new career, the second tragedy occurred in John's young life. He was diagnosed with consumption (tuberculosis), and although he consulted a number of doctors, they all came to the same conclusion: at best, he only had a few months to live. It was unanimously agreed, however, that he might prolong his life if he moved to a drier climate out west.

John immediately packed up his belongings and headed for Dallas, Texas, which was as far as the railroad went at that time. In October 1873, he found a position as dental associate to Dr. John Seegar. As John hung out his shingle and prepared for business, he felt more optimistic about life, but his illness still lingered, and frequent coughing spells wracked his thin body once again. When these episodes happened more and more while he was attending to a tooth extraction or a filling on a patient, he began to lose customers at a rapid rate. He realized he would have to find another way to make a living.

He started to frequent the gambling halls and, before

too long, found he had a natural talent for gambling. In fact, he was so good at it that he decided he might make a reasonable living as a professional gambler. Of course, in those days gamblers had to be able to protect themselves at all times by carrying a gun, so Holliday learned how to use a six-gun and wield a knife. By western standards, however, he made a somewhat strange "gunman." A man who could speak Latin fluently, could play the piano with finesse, had the manners of a southern gentleman, and was a sharp dresser, did not exactly fit the image.

However, on January 2, 1875, despite his education and his appearance, he became involved in his first altercation with a saloonkeeper named Austin, and the scuffle turned violent. Each man drew his gun, firing off several shots, none of which thankfully met their mark. Both Holliday and Austin were arrested, but then released. Witnesses considered the whole affair slightly amusing because both men were such bad shots. However, a few days later Holliday's aim was a little better when, once again his quick temper resulted in an argument with a prominent citizen in Dallas. The two shots he fired left the man very dead, and Holliday was forced to leave town in a hurry ahead of an angry posse.

He stopped off in Jacksboro and found a job dealing faro — a popular card game in 19th century gambling houses, which had originated in France. It consisted of a player betting against a banker (or dealer) on two drawn cards. Holliday soon became even more proficient with his guns, carrying one in a shoulder holster and one on his hip. He also toted a very long knife, always at the ready. His reputation as an expert gunfighter began to grow and, as there was little or no reputable law enforcement in the west at that time, Holliday always managed to escape punishment. However, in yet another gunfight in the summer of 1876, Holliday shot and killed a soldier. This was a big mistake, because now the United States government was also after him.

By the time he finally left Texas, heading through Apache country towards Colorado, he had enraged not only the government, but also the army, the Texas Rangers, and many United States Marshals. He knew that if he were caught by any one of them, he would undoubtedly be hung. He eventually reached Colorado, stopping briefly at various places, such as Pueblo, Leadville, Georgetown, and Central City to make some money gambling.

But Doc Holliday had a quick temper, which he kept on a very short leash; along the way, three more men who had dared to cross him fell victim to his proficiency with a gun. He was living a wild and reckless life, but he knew he would die soon anyway, so it hardly mattered if the law killed him first. His coughing spells were growing worse, and by the time he reached Denver, he was weak and debilitated. He decided to stop there for a while and rest. Going by the name of Tom Mackay, he took a job again dealing faro at the famous Babbitt's House in Denver.

All was going well, until once more Holliday became

embroiled in an argument, this time with a man named Bud Ryan. Holliday would never admit that he might be wrong when he was challenged, and the argument soon turned into a fight. Holliday quickly whisked out his knife and slashed Ryan's face and neck, mutilating him badly. Although Ryan did not die, the people of Denver were incensed by this vicious crime, and Holliday once again had to leave town in a hurry, before an angry mob attacked him and lynched him from the nearest tree.

Holliday drifted through Wyoming for a while and then back to Texas, where he ended up in Fort Griffin and found a job at Shanssey's Saloon, dealing cards. It was there that he met the woman who was to become the love of his life. Their on-again, off-again affair lasted a number of years, despite many violent arguments. It was a fiery and passionate relationship between two people who were both equally stubborn and had similar, irritable dispositions. For once, Holliday had met his match.

Her name was Mary Catherine (Kate) Haroney, and she was born in Hungary in 1850, the daughter of a physician. Her father brought the family to Mexico in 1862 when he was appointed to be the personal surgeon to Emperor Maximilian, Archduke of the Austro-Hungarian Hapsburg Empire. Three years later, the empire crumbled, and the Haroney family was forced to flee Mexico. They settled in Iowa, but that same year, Kate's mother and father both died. Kate was barely fifteen when she and her siblings were placed in foster homes. Kate decided to run away from home and stow away on a steamship bound for St. Louis. The ship's captain allowed her to stay in St. Louis, and there she was placed in a convent school.

She married soon after leaving school, ironically to a dentist, giving birth a year later. Tragically, both her husband and her newborn child died within weeks of one another. Forced to make a living for herself, Kate headed for Kansas. By 1874, she was working in a "sporting house" owned and run by Nellie Earp, the wife of one of Wyatt Earp's brothers. The following year, she worked as a dance hall girl in Dodge City and then headed south to Fort Griffin, Texas, where she dealt cards at John Shanssey's Saloon. And there she met Doc Holliday.

The rocky relationship between Holliday and Kate (often referred to as "Big Nose Kate" because of this prominent feature on an otherwise attractive woman,) was made worse because Kate insisted on being independent. She liked earning her own living, often by plying her trade as a prostitute. She claimed she would belong to no man, and even refused to work for a madam at any of the many bordellos, but preferred to be her own boss and work independently. Her lifestyle infuriated Holliday, and invariably their arguments were caused by Kate's difficulty in staying faithful to him.

Around the same time, Holliday also met Wyatt Earp, who was to have a great influence on his life. Earp had ridden into Fort Griffin from Dodge City, where he was the appointed marshal. He was on the trail of Dave Rudabaugh, a man wanted for train robbery. Holliday agreed to help Earp track the man down, and Earp had great respect for Holliday and his abilities. He did not agree with many others who considered Doc Holliday to be simply a cold-blooded killer. Earp understood his new friend and accepted the fact that he was a hot-headed man with a violent temper, who stood aside for no man.

Soon after this, Kate proved her great love for Doc Holliday. A man named Ed Bailey arrived in Fort Griffin and offered to play poker with Holliday. He was obviously trying to irritate Holliday, to see if his temper was really as bad as it was reported to be. He kept picking up discarded cards and looking through them, which was against the rules of western poker. Holliday warned Bailey twice that if he continued to do this, he would forfeit the pot, but Bailey ignored the warnings. On the next hand, he again picked up the cards that had been discarded and started to look through them.

Without another word, Holliday raked in the pot and refused to show his own hand, so Bailey drew out his gun. In the blink of an eye, Holliday's knife suddenly materialized and before Bailey could fire a shot, Holliday had fatally slashed him. Blood spilled everywhere, and Bailey lay dead, face-down across the table.

Holliday felt he was in the right, so instead of running from the law, he allowed himself to be arrested, believing in his own mind that he was innocent, or at least had been justified in killing the man. There were plenty of witnesses to back him up, after all. His decision to stick around, however, was a big mistake. He was immediately disarmed and held in jail. Bailey's friends demanded Holliday be turned over to them so that they could hang him from the nearest tree. Kate realized that to save further bloodshed, the local law would probably agree and release Holliday to the mob. She had to do something — and fast!

Without giving the matter a second thought, she set fire to an old shed near the jail. It began to burn and the flames spread to other buildings, soon threatening the whole town. Everyone rushed to put out the fire and save the town from being engulfed. Everyone, that is, except Kate, Holliday, and the guard who was watching him. As soon as the whole town was occupied trying to extinguish the fire, Kate stepped inside the jail, a pistol in each hand. She quickly disarmed the guard and passed a pistol over to Holliday, and the two lovers made a hasty retreat. That night, they hid in the brush outside of town and the next morning, headed for Dodge City, 400 miles away, on stolen horses.

Perhaps they decided to head for Dodge because Holliday always felt safe near his friend, Wyatt Earp. In any event, as soon as they arrived in Dodge, Holliday and Kate registered at Deacon Cox's Boarding House under the names of Dr. and Mrs. J. H. Holliday, and Holliday vowed to repay his lady love by finally settling down and devoting his life to making her happy. He gave up gambling and hung out his shingle as a dentist once again. He promised to lead a respectable life if she would promise to stop being a prostitute. In one of their rare on-again, in-love periods, Kate readily agreed, and they began to enjoy a quiet, respectable lifestyle.

Needless to say, however, Kate soon grew bored with the quiet life and told Holliday she was going back to the dance halls and the excitement she had always found in the gambling dens. Once again, the lovers split up and went their separate ways. It would not, however, be the last time their paths would cross.

In September of that year, word reached Holliday at the Long Branch Saloon, where he was back dealing faro, that several Texas cowboys had arrived and had cornered Wyatt Earp on the outskirts of town, intending to shoot him. Holliday immediately took off to help his friend, gun at the ready.

When he arrived, two outlaws were holding Earp at gunpoint, trying to goad him into drawing his gun, while their friends stood by taunting him with insulting remarks. Holliday came up from behind them, shouting out a stream of profanities, which momentarily put them off guard and made them turn around. This maneuver gave Earp just enough time to hit one of them over the head with his long barrel gun. The other cowboys were then promptly relieved of their guns in a peaceful manner, and the moment ended safely. But Wyatt Earp would never forget that his friend, Doc Holliday, had saved his life that night. Their firm friendship became even stronger.

During 1878 and 1879, Holliday and Kate had more reconciliations and break-ups, and after one violent quarrel, Holliday rode off towards Trinidad, Colorado, where he became embroiled in yet another gunfight with a young gambler known as Kid Colton. Colton died in the encounter, so Holliday rode off once again heading for New Mexico. For one summer, he attempted his skills as a dentist yet again. This was to be his last attempt at dentistry; his fatal illness was still consuming his life.

Before leaving New Mexico, his temper got the better of him one more time, causing him to argue with and shoot at a local gunman named Mike Gordon. A mob gathered and tried to hold Holliday so that they could lynch him, but Doc was one step ahead and lit out of town in a cloud of dust. He was by then a lonely, miserable, and embittered man. He headed back to Dodge City where he knew Wyatt Earp's presence would offer him some solace. Much to his despair, when he arrived in Dodge, he found that Wyatt had left, and word was that he had gone to a place called Tombstone in Arizona. Holliday decided to head there also.

It seemed that not only Wyatt, but most of his family, had gone to Tombstone that year. Virgil Earp had already been made a deputy U.S. marshal there. Morgan Earp arrived in town from Montana, and Wyatt and James Earp arrived from Dodge City. Holliday, himself, stopped along the way at a place called Prescott, where he met up with Kate once more and began to have incredible luck at the gambling tables.

They stayed on a while. Then, in the summer of 1880, he and Kate left Prescott together with $40,000 in winnings and also headed for Tombstone.

Once again Kate's independent nature encouraged her to make her own money, so she rounded up some willing females, bought some cheap whiskey and opened Tombstone's first "sporting house" in a large tent.

There were many outlaws in Tombstone at that time, all of whom resented the Earps and Doc Holliday being there. Most prominent among the troublemakers were "Old Man" Clanton and his sons, Ike, Phin, and Billy; and the McLaury brothers, Frank and Tom. Bill Brocius, John Ringo, and Frank Stilwell were also in town and all were wild, dangerous men. For most of the year leading up to a standoff in October 1881, tension grew between the "law" and the "cowboys." At the same time as things were heating up in Tombstone, Holliday and Kate were continuing their fiercely passionate and oft times anger-filled relationship. It was a love-hate relationship neither one of them seemed able to do without. It seemed they could not live together in harmonious bliss for very long, but they could not live without one another, either.

Meanwhile, the long expected confrontation between the two factions in town finally came to a head on October 26, 1881. It was all over in 30 seconds, and yet it was to become the single most famous gunfight in western history. It took place in a vacant lot near the intersection of Third and Fremont Streets, alongside a boarding house and photo studio. Wyatt, his brothers Virgil and Morgan, and Doc Holliday were on one side, while the Clantons, the McLaurys, and Billy Claiborne were on the other. The location of the shootout was actually directly *behind* the OK Corral and not *in* it, but it took that name and was immortalized forever as the "Gunfight at the OK Corral." In the encounter, both of Wyatt's brothers and Doc Holliday were wounded, while Billy Clanton, and Frank and Tom McLaury were killed.

Wyatt Earp, Doc Holliday, and Earp's brothers were all arrested by the sheriff for murder, but their subsequent trial proved that they had acted within the law and had merely attempted to control the unruly outlaw element in town.

The aftermath of that tragic day in history, however, left a trail of blood through Arizona. Revenge was sought on many levels. In January of 1882, John Ringo challenged Wyatt and Holliday, but it was mostly the whisky talking, and nothing came of his challenge. In March, however, while Morgan Earp, having recovered from his wound, was playing pool at Hatch's Saloon on Allen Street, a shot fired through the open window from the dark alley outside struck Morgan in the back, as it was intended to do. He died immediately.

Wyatt went on a rampage, knowing the men who were behind his brother's death. He first killed Frank Stilwell at the Tucson Station on March 20. A judge issued a warrant for Earp's arrest along with that of Doc Holliday, but Wyatt Earp was unconcerned. He said that the killing of Stilwell was just the beginning of what he and Doc Holliday intended to do to avenge all the deaths of innocent men and, at the same time, eliminate the outlaw regime that ruled the west. He considered himself on the side of the law and, as such, had to do what must be done. He and Holliday headed out of town to round up more outlaws and they first came upon Florentino Cruz, a gang member. Under pressure, Cruz squealed on the others who had been involved in the murder of Morgan Earp. Earp and Holliday shot them all on the spot on March 22. Two days later, Curly Bill Brocius was also shot, and Johnny Barnes another outlaw received a serious wound from which he never recovered.

Over the next year, the list of cowboy outlaws eliminated by the guns of Wyatt Earp and Doc Holliday grew. The two men were hell bent on a bloody trail of vengeance, and nothing stood in their way. When they finally left Tombstone for good, having satisfied themselves that most of the criminal element had been struck down, they rode off towards Silver City, New Mexico, where they sold their horses, rode a stage to Deeming, and then boarded a train back to Colorado.

Upon arrival in Denver, Doc Holliday was arrested by Perry Mallan for past crimes there. Some people claimed that Mallan was actually the brother of an old enemy of Holliday who had been run out of Tombstone. Mallan was seeking his own revenge. Holliday was temporarily placed in jail, but on May 22, 1882, the *Denver Republican* ran the following announcement:

Holliday has a big reputation as a fighter, and has probably put more rustlers and cowboys under the sod than any other one man in the west. He had been the terror of the lawless element in Arizona, and with the Earps was the only man brave enough to face the bloodthirsty crowd which has made the name of Arizona a stench in the nostrils of decent men.

After Mallan claimed to have been a witness to Holliday's killing of Curly Bill Brocius, Holliday retorted with the remark that "if Mallan was alongside Curly Bill when he was killed that day, he was with one of the worst gangs of murderers and robbers in the country." Public opinion demanded that Holliday be released. By the end of May, Doc Holliday's legal problems concerning extradition in Arizona were also finally resolved by the governor, so Holliday was cleared of all crimes he may or may not have committed.

He left Denver and headed for Pueblo again and then on to Leadville, where he ran into two old enemies from Tombstone: Billy Allen and Johnny Tyler. Allen had been looking for Holliday with a gun, and around 5 o'clock on the evening of August 19, 1884, Doc Holliday was involved in his last gunfight.

He had wandered into Hyman's Saloon and sat down at the end of the bar. Friends had warned Holliday that Allen was gunning for him, so as Allen came across the threshold, Holliday aimed his pistol at him and fired. The bullet creased Allen's head, so Holliday shot him once more, this time through the left arm. Witnesses then disarmed Holliday, because they knew that Allen was not yet dead and he would have retaliated. Holliday, however, was later acquitted of the shooting charges, as there were many witnesses who claimed to have heard Allen threatening him. Although Holliday went through the legal process for this last crime, his popularity and public sentiment again won the day. He was a free man.

In the winter of 1885, Holliday returned to Denver where he met up with his old friend, Wyatt Earp, in the lobby of the Windsor Hotel. By then, Holliday's condition had deteriorated badly. He had a continuous cough and stood on unsteady legs, but the two men enjoyed one last drink together.

By May of 1887, Holliday's health was at its lowest point. He then heard of the so-called magical sulfur vapors at Glenwood Springs, which might help his condition. He did not believe in miracles, but was prepared to try anything, so he headed out for Glenwood Springs and registered at the Hotel Glenwood. There is some evidence to prove that Kate was with him at the hotel and that she took care of him and all their expenses during Holliday's last 57 days. He was delirious for many of them, but on the morning of November 8, 1887, he awoke feeling better, his mind clear, and his delirium gone. He asked Kate for a glass of whiskey, which she handed to him. He drained the glass and smiled at her as he looked down the bed at his bare feet.

"This is funny," he said. Holliday had always expected he would "die with his boots on" as a result of a gunshot wound, a knife in the ribs, or possibly at the end of a rope. They were his last words. He died peacefully shortly afterwards. This was not the way Holliday had planned on going. After all, he once claimed that he had almost lost his life a total of nine times. Four attempts had been made to hang him, and he was shot at in a gunfight or ambush five times. The final count was most probably a whole lot higher.

Kate took care of everything during the last two months that Holliday was bedridden and, when he died, she arranged for his possessions to be shipped to his family in Georgia. His funeral was held in Glenwood Cemetery, and his obituary, which appeared in the Leadville *Carbonate Chronicle* on November 14, 1887, stated, among other things, that "Doc Holliday enjoyed the reputation of being one of the most fearless men on the frontier."

Kate stayed on in Colorado, and apparently married in Aspen, in 1888. She and her husband, George Cummings, eventually moved back to Arizona, and Kate reverted to her birth name of Mary while she worked as a cook in the mining camps there. The marriage only lasted until 1899, when she left her alcoholic husband and worked as a housekeeper in Dos Cabezas until 1931. She then lied about her place of birth, saying she was born in Iowa, so that she would become eligible to enter the Arizona State Pioneers' Home, where she lived until her death on November 2, 1940. She is buried under the name of Mary Katherine Cummings in the Arizona Pioneers Cemetery in Prescott, Arizona.

There is a certain irony connected to where the famous Doc Holliday is buried and it is one that he would most probably have enjoyed. The Glenwood Springs cemetery is situated on a high hill overlooking a valley. At the time of his death in 1887, the steep road leading to the cemetery was covered in ice and too treacherous to travel. He was therefore buried at the foot of the hill and the intention was to move his body into the cemetery when the ice thawed. Unfortunately, this never happened.

Many years later, a housing development was built at the base of the hill so, although a tombstone marker with Doc's name on it sits up in the cemetery, his actual remains probably lie in someone's back yard in the valley.

Chapter 5
Denver's Most Notorious Madam

L ittle Mattie Silks stood all of five feet tall. Her rotund figure with its ample bosom adorned in the finest of silk material, showed a flamboyance and determination as she was handed a revolver by her second. She eyed her opponent, Kate Fulton, with suspicion. The two women were both in the same profession, the oldest in the west, and both owned bordellos in late-1870s Denver. On that particular day, they were about to compete in the first (and possibly only) duel fought in the west between women.

An earlier argument, when Mattie had accused Kate of shooting at her carriage and being too friendly with her lover, Cortez Thomson, had been overheard by many people. Mattie had challenged Kate to a duel. The whole town turned out to witness the proceedings.

The atmosphere was tense as the women were told to pace off before firing. Both followed their instructions to the letter, as though this were common practice for them. Fortunately, however, Mattie and Kate were atrocious shots, and neither of their bullets hit their intended mark. Mattie's, in fact, accidentally grazed the neck of her lover, Thomson, who was watching the proceedings on the sidelines. Although he was unhurt, Mattie was devastated.

News of the duel was reported in the newspapers over the coming weeks, and each report was more exaggerated than the last. One reporter even wrote that both the dueling madams were naked to the waist when they squared off against one another! A few days after the duel, Kate attacked Mattie once again, but this time she was hauled away by the law, and peace was once again restored in the red-light district of Denver. In any event, Mattie was not complaining. As a result of all the publicity, her business increased by leaps and bounds.

Mattie was born in either 1846 or 1848 in Terre Haute, Indiana, or in Kansas, or possibly even in Buffalo, New York. Each time she talked of her past, her story varied. Mattie claimed to have grown up on a farm and knew from an early age that she wanted to become a madam and have her own fancy bordello. Her wish to become a madam without ever having to prostitute herself seems to be true, because by the time she was 19, she had already opened and was running her first bordello in Springfield, Illinois. She soon realized, however, that the really big money for women working at the oldest trade in the world, was out west, so by the mid-1870s, Mattie was determined to move on.

In order to make money to pay for her trip west, she worked hard at any job she could find, including being a freighter for many of the wagon trains heading to Colorado from Missouri. She also began to gather a group of women around her (known then as soiled doves) who came from the mining camps of Abilene and Dodge City, promising them that she would take care of them if they worked for her. She told them stories of how she planned one day to own the fanciest, grandest houses in Colorado, and how they would all reap the benefits from the money she would make. As they made their way to the Colorado gold mining towns, Mattie and her girls stopped occasionally to set up a canvas tent in which the girls plied their trade.

In 1875, Mattie's entourage arrived in Georgetown, Colorado and, true to her word, Mattie was soon the owner of a bordello from which she made a handsome profit. She also met a man named Silks in Georgetown, and apparently a common law marriage of some kind took place between the two. Although Mattie took his name, there is no record of any legal marriage. In any event, two years later, Mattie left Georgetown and Silks forever, declaring she liked his name more than she liked him. For the rest of her life she kept the name Silks, and it remained something of a symbol for her, because she would always adorn herself in the finest of silk gowns.

Not long after she arrived in Denver with her girls in 1877, she made newspaper headlines. According to the *Rocky Mountain News,* "Madame Silks was fined $12 for drunkenness, and paid it like a little woman. She ought to play it finer when she gets on a spree."

But little Mattie enjoyed her whiskey and liked to have a good time. She kept a small revolver hidden on her person at all times for protection. Needless to say, her flamboyant lifestyle made her the subject of many a scandal, including the infamous duel with competing madam, Kate Fulton.

The event occurred soon after Mattie fell in love with Cortez Thomson. Unfortunately, Thomson was something of a ladies' man and also had a wife and daughter back east. That, however, did not deter Mattie from showering her affections on him. During the Civil War, Cortez Thomson had ridden with Quantrill's raiders, a tough bunch of gunmen, but when Mattie met him, he was a well known sprinter in town as well as being a Denver volunteer fireman. On the particular day in question, a race was taking place that had drawn a large audience west of the city limits. Most people had come specifically to see Thomson run, because he always wore bright pink tights and star-spangled blue trunks, and presented quite a figure. Mattie, of course, had placed a large bet on her lover, and when he won the race, the pair began to celebrate.

Mattie soon got into an argument with Kate Fulton, who claimed that Mattie had stolen Thomson from her. According to a newspaper account, Thomson stepped forward, told Kate she was a liar, and hit her squarely on the nose. Kate's latest man, Sam Thatcher, stepped in and defended his woman. In the process, he also was hit by Thomson. The celebrations were now ruined, so Mattie and Thomson headed for their carriage and left the scene to return to town. Suddenly, a second carriage pulled up alongside them and a gun was fired, the bullet barely missing Thomson. Mattie was incensed, accused Kate, and vowed revenge.

She challenged Kate to a duel to settle the affair. Whatever the truth really was about the supposed duel, Mattie was delighted by its outcome. She loved publicity and, for the next 20 years, she was the reigning queen and ran the finest of establishments, with a client list that included government officials and the leading Denver businessmen. Mattie Silks was indeed the accepted Queen of Market Street.

Although she possessed an excellent head for business, Mattie's personal taste in men was questionable at best. When Cortez Thomson's wife back east died, he proposed to Mattie, and she accepted immediately. The two were married in July 1884. Two years later, Thomson's daughter also died, leaving behind a small child. Thomson wanted nothing to do with his grandchild, but Mattie felt otherwise and adopted the child herself and agreed to take care of her.

Of course, Thomson now had access to all Mattie's wealth

Mattie Silks and another woman pose outdoors
with Mattie Silks' horse in Denver, Colorado.

and, in return, Mattie inherited a hard-drinking, gambling
womanizer who was only too happy to spend her money. He
purchased a ranch near Wray, Colorado, with Mattie's money
and her blessing: Mattie herself bought the best horses for the
ranch. She took frequent holidays at the ranch, but remained
in Denver most of the time to run her many businesses.
Whenever Thomson visited her, he was usually drunk and
only came to town for more money to lose at gambling.

None of this seemed to matter to Mattie. She was happy as the reigning Queen of Market Street and she continued to play the madam and to buy up more real estate. She also sold one of her houses (at 2009 Market Street) to her friend Jennie Roger, a rival madam. Both women respected one another and managed to stay friends in the same business, despite a certain rivalry. As a couple, they made an odd sight: petite, dumpy Mattie and six-foot tall, Jenny. Mattie wore silks, while Jenny always sported long, emerald earrings, which emphasized her height.

Despite their friendship, Jennie owned one thing that Mattie envied and wanted badly — the famous House of Mirrors at 1942 Market Street. The House of Mirrors was the most elegant of Colorado "cat" houses, and carved into its facade were the busts of the men Jenny supposedly had blackmailed in order to build this mausoleum. It originally had a dining room, three parlors, a large ballroom area, a wine cellar, and at least 15 bedrooms. There were also mirrors on all the ceilings, a grand piano, a golden harp, and numerous chandeliers throughout. The maple woodwork inside was set off by expensive oriental rugs. For a while, Jennie even dethroned Mattie from her coveted position of queen bee, but even that did not harm their friendship.

In April of 1900, Mattie's husband, Thomson, became seriously ill out at their ranch. Mattie immediately rushed out of town to be by his side and nurse him back to health but, sadly, he died the next day. Mattie was broken-hearted.

Despite his many faults, Thomson was her one true love. She arranged for his body to be buried in style at the famous Fairmount Cemetery in Denver.

After a suitable period of mourning, Mattie returned to her business on Market Street, but within a few years, a social movement grew up that threatened to close down all the houses of ill repute along the Row. Mattie was unperturbed; she knew there would always be a need for the services she provided. Each year, she would go back east to recruit new talent and brought girls back to Denver, first parading them through the streets to attract new business. Mattie was popular with all those who worked for her, because she treated them well, allowing them to keep half of whatever they made. She also served them two ample meals daily, breakfast at 11.30 a.m and dinner at 5 p.m.

When her friend, Jennie, died in 1909, Mattie paid $14,000 in cash to Jennie's estate in order to purchase the infamous House of Mirrors. Now she could really reclaim her title and brandish her notoriety to everyone. She even had the words "M. Silks" engraved in the tile floor at the front entrance of that grand establishment.

Her business continued to do well, despite prohibition, which took hold in 1915. She hired handsome Jack Ready to be her financial adviser and bouncer. Before long, the two became lovers and, at the age of 76, in the early 1920s, Mattie married Jack, a man many years her junior. To keep abreast of the times, which were changing rapidly, they both decided to turn one of her houses into a respectable hotel. This allowed Mattie to continue in the business world.

Mattie, however, had been forced to sell the fabulous House of Mirrors in 1919, and the heart of her business had gone. She no longer had the energy or the ambition she once had and was eventually quite happy to retire with Jack to her ranch in Wray. Mattie was content with her lot in life. She had made enough money to live comfortably and had never had to prostitute herself to do it.

Mattie Silks (now known as the respectable Martha Ready) died in the Denver General Hospital in 1929, following complications after a fall. There were few mourners at her funeral. Her last request had been to be buried next to Cortez Thomson, her one true love. Her estate was then divided between Jack Ready and her adopted granddaughter. Jack Ready died two years later.

Following Mattie's sale of the legendary House of Mirrors in 1919, it remained a house of prostitution until the early 1930s, at which time moral reform dictated the demise of the red-light district completely. The house later became a Buddhist Temple and then, for many years, was a warehouse. The face of Market Street had radically changed.

Today, the building has been restored to its original beauty and operates as a restaurant and a nightclub. It is often booked for private functions, such as class reunions and weddings. But the house that was once described as "the brothel of all brothels" is said to still be inhabited by a few ghosts from its past.

Many people claim to have felt a presence around them when no one can be seen. Staff often smell cigar smoke and claim they hear women's high heels walking over the wooden floors upstairs when the restaurant is closed. Occasionally a wineglass and ashtray is left on a table that had previously been cleared. Sometimes the lights dim for no apparent reason. Electricians claim there is no faulty connection. A piano is said to play by itself on the second floor and occasionally whispers and giggles are heard behind closed doors when rooms are empty.

Psychics claim that Jennie Rogers, the original owner of the House of Mirrors, haunts the upstairs, while Mattie Silks occupies the main-floor area, which is now the restaurant. Another story claims that a man and woman committed suicide in one of the upstairs rooms, and their spirits are also said to haunt the establishment. At least six spirits have been identified by those who believe in such things and are said to haunt the building at various times. The sound of laughter, breaking glass, and the experience of having someone brush against you when no one is there all add to the mystery and make the House of Mirrors a popular stopping place for ghost storytellers on the *Gunslingers, Ghosts, and Gold* ghost tour in downtown Denver today.

One thing is for sure. Mattie Silks, the little girl from Indiana, achieved her dream of becoming the most famous madam in the west, the owner of the grandest bordello in downtown Denver — and she did it all without ever having to be a prostitute herself.

Today she lies buried in Fairmount Cemetery, Denver, under a headstone that reads "Martha Ready." It's hard to believe she was once the toast of Market Street's red-light district in Denver, and that her elegant houses of ill repute were famous throughout the state of Colorado.

Chapter 6
The Bad Seed

hen the prison warden, accompanied by two guards, came for Jimmy Melton on June 27, 1973, they found him hiding beneath his cot in his small cell. He was trembling violently. He begged them to leave him there. It was the only place he felt really safe; he had, after all, spent the best part of his life behind bars. But that day he was supposed to be released back into the world, and Jimmy did not want to go.

The warden left him alone while he decided what should be done. When Jimmy was sure they had gone, he came out from his hiding place and sat on the cot. His thoughts once more took him back to Christmas 1947, when it all began. At that time, he and his older sister, Phyllis, lived with their father near Las Animas. Their mother had deserted them.

Jimmy still remembered it all so clearly. He recalled how the lights on the Christmas tree twinkled brightly and everything in the room looked so normal. It was December 16, and Jimmy was watching his sister as he sat cross-legged on the floor opposite her. He tried to close his ears to what she was saying, but her voice grated on his nerves and was giving him a headache. She looked at an old photograph album as she nagged him about the chores he still had to do before Christmas.

"You have to help me wrap these presents, too, Jimmy," she said. "I can't do everything by myself."

He hated it when she tried to play the role of mother. She was only four years older than he was, after all, but she kept reminding him that because Mamma had gone and left them all, it was her responsibility to look out for Jimmy. She was the mother in the family now. She had to help Pa, so Jimmy must be a good boy and do as he was told. At 16, Phyllis Melton enjoyed her position of power.

Jimmy stood up slowly, no longer listening to his sister's voice, drowned out now by the voices in his head. Yes, everything was normal on the outside, but inside Jimmy's head there was turmoil. Why had his mother left them? Why was his father now so angry and miserable all the time? And what gave Phyllis the right to order him about? Suddenly, he snapped. He still remembered it clearly. He walked towards Pa's desk and opened the top drawer. It was usually kept locked, because that was where Pa kept his .22 caliber gun.

The night before, Jimmy had noticed that for some reason Pa had forgotten to lock the drawer. He hoped that there were bullets in the gun or in a box beside it in the drawer. It would only take a second to load the gun, and he knew how to do it because he had often watched his father.

Pa had told them the gun was just there for their protection, in case they were ever robbed. Living out on the farm in Las Animas, they were far from town; and you never knew who might stop by, Pa always said. "Well," thought Jimmy, "right now I am being robbed of my peace of mind, so I need to use the gun."

"What'yer doing, Jimmy?" said Phyllis. "Come over here and look at this picture of Mamma and me. See how she's holding me so tight. See how she loved me. It must have been 'cos of you that she left."

Jimmy turned and walked towards her slowly and deliberately. Then she looked up. "Jimmy Melton!" she screamed at him. "Put down that gun right now! Pa'll have your hide."

Jimmy smiled sadistically as he cocked the gun and fired at her. He fired 11 more times, until he was sure she was dead. He was amazed by the amount of blood that splattered all over the carpet, the photo album, the unwrapped presents, and even the Christmas tree. Phyllis was slumped face down in that blood, her throat gurgling as she took her last breath. Then there was silence.

"She will never nag me again," Jimmy thought. "I'm free." He sat down calmly in an armchair and waited. The voices inside his head had finally stopped.

Jimmy started trembling again as he sat on the prison cot so many years later. The memories were still so vivid. He wished he could forget. It was only later, when people began to care about him again, that he had found some sort of peace.

Eventually, Jimmy had come out of his trance-like state on that December night. He realized he must do something quickly. He decided he would hide Phyllis's body in the basement, but he needed to wrap something around her so he wouldn't drag blood everywhere. He found a blanket and began his task, but he wasn't thinking too clearly. He got blood all over himself by the time he had dragged his sister down the basement stairs. But then he thought that would look good, because he would tell his father that someone had broken in and attacked them both. Yes, that story sounded good.

By the time his father got home, Jimmy Melton had his story straight. He told him that two men had broken into the house wearing masks. They were looking for money, he claimed. They beat him and took Phyllis away by force. That was all he knew. His father immediately telephoned the police, imagining his daughter had been kidnapped for ransom. He was not a rich man, though, just a part-time farmer and a full-time owner of the local hardware store. Why would anyone want to kidnap *his* daughter?

The police were also suspicious and did not believe Jimmy's story. There was so much blood in the living room, and yet Jimmy did not appear to be hurt. Despite the obvious, he kept insisting he had been beaten. After 24 hours of intensive questioning, Jimmy finally broke down and admitted that he had killed his sister and that her body was hidden in the basement.

"I never liked her very much," he shouted. "She was always nagging me to do things, so I shot her to keep her quiet."

Jimmy's father was shocked and heartbroken. How could he have sired such a vicious killer? He already knew the boy had problems, though. Jimmy was a slightly-built boy who wore glasses and appeared to be quiet and studious, but he had occasionally shown a vicious temper in the past. He was angry about his parents divorcing and his mother running off. But this? To murder his own sister in cold blood? To James Melton, Senior, it was inconceivable. Nonetheless, Jimmy had committed murder and, at that time, Colorado only had two facilities for the incarceration of young boys. Murderers, no matter how old, were automatically sent to the penitentiary.

Jimmy was interviewed by psychiatrists at the Colorado Psychopathic Hospital, where he was advised to plead guilty by reason of insanity. Efforts were also made for Jimmy to be accepted into Father Flanagan's Boys' Town, an organization that helped wayward juveniles reassess their lives, repent their sins, and go on to live better lives. But following his brief stay at the hospital, and with no word from Father Flanagan as to whether or not he would be admitted, Jimmy pleaded guilty to second-degree murder and, following his conviction, was sent to Canon City penitentiary.

Jimmy still remembered arriving at the penitentiary in 1948 and meeting the warden, Roy Best. Best agreed that Jimmy should be mugged and fingerprinted, but refused to allow him to spend even one night in the prison. He declared, "If this boy is to come out of this as a decent citizen, he must have the same advantages as other boys — insofar as they are possible under the circumstances. He won't get them behind bars with the toughs I've got in here."

Roy Best was a unique man. He had come to the Canon City Penitentiary at one of the worst times in the prison's history, right after the 1929 riot, one of the most destructive in prison history. His father, Boone Best, had also served a term as warden for a few short months prior to his death. Roy had grown up on a cattle ranch near Rocky Ford, Colorado, and started life as a performing bronco buster. He even ran his own Wild West Show in New York for a while and had performed in Madison Square Garden.

As a prison warden, he was a straightforward, free-thinking man, who listened to what people had to say. He respected honesty and frankness. He was credited with rebuilding the prison complex at minimal cost, bearing in mind the safety of the guards and making sure prisoners were living in a clean environment. Prisoners respected him because he was tough. His philosophy was "Discipline without Tyranny;" he believed all prisoners, no matter what their crime, were human beings first and, as such, deserved respect. He was, however, a strict disciplinarian and could at times be cruel if he thought it necessary.

When he first met young Jimmy Melton, he felt certain that, with the right guidance, this boy could be led down a better path — but certainly not in a prison. To the system, Jimmy was simply prisoner No. 24939, but to Roy Best, he was a young boy crying out for help.

With this in mind, Best asked that the boy be released into his custody so that he and his wife could take him into their own home, look after him, and make sure he got a good education. Newspaper reporters had a field day with that. Never before had a warden taken such an interest in a prisoner. A kindly warden giving a young thug a second chance was unheard of. *Life Magazine* ran a long article entitled, "WARDEN ADOPTS A YOUNG MURDERER: BOY SHOT HIS SISTER IS GIVEN A CHANCE TO LEAD A NORMAL LIFE" in their April 12, 1948 edition. They even ran a photograph showing Jimmy reading himself to sleep with a copy of *Black Beauty* in his hands.

While living with Roy Best and his wife, Jimmy settled into a good life. He was initially enrolled in public school, but other parents in Canon City did not want their children associating with a murderer, so Best paid for a private home tutor named Verna Heaton. She taught him the importance of studying hard to make something of himself, and Best insisted that he work hard, be conscientious, and do all his home chores, as well as school work. He believed that "Jimmy [is] a fine boy, just like a son, and in the last six months he has been here, he has never done anything to make us want to put him back in a cell." Jimmy was even allowed to play sports and learn piano. He joined the Episcopal Church and became an altar boy. Jimmy smiled to himself just thinking back to those happy days, and he figured that his transformation from cold-blooded killer to innocent altar boy was nothing short of miraculous.

Jimmy might well have continued on this path and made something of his life, but within a year of coming into the Meltons' home, Roy Best's wife died. Jimmy no longer had a mother figure to care for him, so Best arranged for Jimmy's admission into Father Flanagan's Boys' Town in Omaha, Nebraska, on March 25, 1949.

Back in 1917, the courts had assigned three orphans to Father Ed Flanagan's care, which made him realize that looking after juveniles and those who needed guidance was a full-time job. He found an old house in Omaha, Nebraska, to shelter the boys and borrowed $90 from a friend to get started. That was the beginning of what eventually became known as Boys' Town.

Soon, two more juvenile delinquents were placed in Father Flanagan's care, but Flanagan believed, "There is no such thing as a bad boy." He strove all his life to turn troubled youth into godly men. He firmly believed that boys who had been deprived of "a mother's tenderness and a father's wisdom, and the love of a family" needed to be compensated in some way. He said on one occasion, "We will never get anywhere in our reform schools and orphan asylums until we compensate for that great loss in young lives."

By 1936, Father Flanagan's community had moved from Omaha to an acreage outside of town called Overlook Farm. His organization was renamed Boys' Town and incorporated as a village. From then on, juvenile court judges and welfare agencies recommended boys to Father Flanagan. Boys' Town was supported entirely by voluntary contributions.

In 1949, Boys' Town seemed the perfect answer for Jimmy Melton, following Mrs. Best's death, and his admission there was granted on March 25 that year. Unfortunately, it lasted only six months. In September, Jimmy fled, claiming the other boys had teased him for being an ex-con. Jimmy didn't feel like a convict. He still felt the Bests had been his family, so he escaped by attacking a visitor with a lead pipe while the man sat in his car. Jimmy then robbed him and took off. This offence landed him in a solitary cell at the Canon City Penitentiary.

This time he spent four years in jail and came up for parole on October 26, 1953. He was released into the custody of his mother and her new husband, who lived in California. His mother, stepfather, and stepsister met him at the prison gates, and they all took off in the family car for Los Angeles to begin a new life. Jimmy was dressed in a $25 suit. He was 18 years old and felt confident that maybe with a new family the bad times were finally over.

His parole board had stated, "The next two or three years are very important in his life from a rehabilitation standpoint. The board feels he has a chance to reform his life and can do it outside under normal circumstances."

However, what were normal circumstances for most people proved far from normal for the still-troubled Jimmy Melton. Even though he was enrolled at the Santa Monica Technical School to carve out a career in auto body repair, he could not resist getting into trouble. In 1954, he left California and headed for Colorado by stealing his mother's 1950 two-door Ford sedan. He abandoned the car and was caught hitchhiking near Kit Carson, carrying an 8-inch hunting knife and a 6-foot length of heavy twine. He admitted to the police that he wanted to kill his father and had returned to Colorado for that purpose.

Once more back in Canon City Penitentiary, it was obvious that Jimmy Melton's problems were far from solved. That same year, Warden Roy Best died, and the prison system lost a great man. Four former Colorado governors and a federal judge formed an honorary escort at his funeral, and in the eulogy Dr. Benjamin Eltelgeroge stated, "Colorado is a far more interesting state because Roy Best lived in it, and the state penitentiary is a far better institution because he ran it." Best's death had an enormous effect on Jimmy. Yet another person he had loved and trusted had left him.

Harry Tinsley was now the acting warden, and it was he who suggested Jimmy's parole again in June of 1957, at which time his parole officer said that Jimmy had made good use of his time in prison and could easily now have a future as a machine operator, a chauffeur, a truck driver, or a book-keeper, if he applied himself. Even Jimmy, now 22 years old, believed he was old enough and wise enough to successfully make his own way in the world.

Wayne Patterson, the state parole director at that time, stated, "This third chance is his last. If it fails, the book is closed." Jimmy was put on parole for life, and part of the agreement was that he get psychiatric counseling to help him succeed in the outside world. He had, after all, spent most of his youth in prison.

Jimmy appeared to be rehabilitated and went to work for the state highway department. He quit in December 1957, after his application to move back to California was granted. Once in California, he took a job as a laborer in a factory, and later told reporters that even though everyone there knew that he was an ex-con, they never held it against him. Things seemed to be going well for Jimmy until one day in March of 1959.

He was arrested in Santa Monica, California for carrying a .38 caliber pistol he had stolen from a gun shop. He was suspected and then charged with being involved in a string of robberies, while in possession of the gun. He denied the charges, but did admit to a drug habit. He knew he was addicted to codeine and benzedrine, which he had first sampled in prison at age 16. This addiction merely compounded his other problems.

In April of 1959 he was returned to Canon City, Colorado, and incarcerated once again to resume his life sentence. Harry Tinsley was now the warden and he encouraged Jimmy not to give up. He, like Roy Best, believed the young man could still make it. Unfortunately, however, Jimmy was denied a fourth parole by the state parole board. Deputy Attorney General Frank Hickey declared "As far as this board is concerned, Melton has struck out for life."

Jimmy's fate was sealed. He would now live out his life as a convict and, in many ways, this suited him just fine. Despite all the help he had received along the way, it seemed that Jimmy was beyond redemption. Then, in April of 1971, now 34 years old and having spent 20 years behind bars, he won yet another parole. This one lasted a mere four days. On April 13, he was arrested by police for writing $425 worth of checks on the business account of the man for whom he had gone to work. With the money, Jimmy had bought expensive champagne to entertain some women he had picked up, obviously trying to make up for lost time. He was back in prison within a week.

Wayne Patterson was warden of the prison when Jimmy Melton was finally about to be discharged from prison for the last time in 1973. He was also going to be discharged from his life parole. But Jimmy now found the thought of a life outside prison unbearable. He sat for a long time in his cell, staring into space and remembering all that had happened to him. He dreaded the warden's return, expecting that he would be forced to leave the only place he thought of as home. When the warden finally returned, however, it was to tell Jimmy that he was being transferred to a mental hospital in Pueblo. The powers-that-be had all agreed that he would never survive in the outside world.

Jimmy's internship in hospital was brief. He hated being held with other mental patients; even the outside world was preferable to that so, soon after being admitted, he made his escape.

And there, the Jimmy Melton story ends. It is believed he made his way back to California, but his whereabouts between June 1973 and his possible death in Los Angeles in 1985 remain a mystery. For 12 years, Jimmy Melton disappeared off the face of the earth. In a perfect world, one would like to suppose that he finally went straight and even repented his vicious crime back in 1947.

Social security records show that a James Melton, whose date of birth differed by only one day from Jimmy Melton "the Boy Killer of Las Animas," died in the Los Angeles area in 1985. He was 50 years old.

Chapter 7
Poker Alice to Her Friends

When well into her 60s, Alice Ivers Tubbs said that she would rather play poker with five or six experts than eat. "And at my age, I probably should be at home knitting, but this is much more fun," she added.

It is hard to believe that Alice Ivers, born in Sudbury, England, in 1853, the only daughter of a schoolteacher, would end her life in Sturgis, South Dakota, having lived for at least 40 of her 77 years as a tough, cigar-chomping, gun-toting gambler. In Colorado, she became one of the greatest poker players and best faro dealers in the west, despite an upbringing that had offered her the education and polish of a young woman of breeding.

Her father had sent her to a women's seminary in

Poker Alice to Her Friends

Sudbury and had always instilled moral values in his daughter. When Alice was 12 years old, the family immigrated to America, settling first in Virginia, where Alice attended a fashionable southern school offering the best in education. With the Civil War at its height and with gold beckoning in the west, the Ivers family moved to Lake City, Colorado.

By then Alice was a beautiful young woman of breeding and class. She attracted the attention of many young men, including Frank Duffield, a mining engineer and gambler, who became her first, and perhaps only, true love. The two were soon married and, because of Frank's work, began to move from one boom mining camp to another, finally settling back in Lake City. The Duffields became the centre of social activity wherever they partied, and Alice enjoyed all the attention she received. She also enjoyed joining Frank at the poker tables, preferring that to staying home. Frank taught her all he knew about the game of poker, and she even sat in on games while Frank was at work. She gained some notoriety, because women were not expected to be poker players — and good ones at that. Alice's education served her well. Her math skills were excellent, and she developed a keen sense for the cards. Before long, she was a far better poker player than her husband and most of his friends.

A few years into their marriage, Frank was tragically killed in a mine explosion, and Alice quickly realized she would now have to make her own way in the world. This did not daunt her, however, because she knew she could easily make a good living as a professional gambler. She felt it had always been her calling in life. After a suitable period of mourning, she returned to the tables and before long was known by one and all as "Poker Alice."

She was soon working the gambling houses in most of Colorado's towns, from Alamosa and Central City to Georgetown and Leadville. Alice liked to dress fashionably and was always neat in appearance. No one would suspect she carried a .38 caliber revolver on her at all times. At some point in her gambling career, she acquired a taste for cigars and from then on was always seen puffing away on her black stogies — not a particularly endearing habit for a woman. If anyone made a comment about it, she pulled out her revolver; the mere sight of it would soon put a stop to any more remarks.

Alice later traveled through Oklahoma, working the gambling tables there. Gradually her fame spread. Never happier than when she was playing against the great card professionals in other houses, she continued to win large amounts of cash. Her greatest pleasure was to actually break the bank. After a particularly long winning streak in Silver City, New Mexico, she headed for New York City and treated herself to an extravagant spree of night-life, shopping for clothes, and enjoying the shows. Once she had spent most of her money, she headed west once again.

Before long, Alice heard about the new mining camp in Creede, Colorado, where fortunes were being made and lost overnight, so she decided to move there in 1890 and get a piece of the action for herself. Now almost 40 years old, she found a job at Bob Ford's Exchange, working eight-hour shifts at the tables. People loved to come and see her, because she was so different from most of the run-of-the-mill women. She spoke in a clipped British accent, enjoyed her whiskey neat, never drank while she gambled, and never, under any circumstances, gambled on Sundays. That was the day she devoted to Bible reading and meditation

Her boss in Creede, Bob Ford, was the man who had killed Jesse James. He had already built a reputation for himself in town, because he liked to tell everyone that he was the James killer. However, because of his boastful ways and the fact that many people still thought of Jesse James as a hero rather than an outlaw, Ford had also made many enemies. When one of them, Ed Kelly, finally shot Ford in 1892, Alice was a witness to the shooting.

Soon after that, she decided to head for Deadwood, South Dakota, where once again she found work in a saloon. The dealer at the next table was a man named Warren Tubbs who hailed from Sturgis. Alice and Tubbs soon became friends. Although Tubbs was not a particularly good poker player, it didn't bother him too much. During the daytime, he made his living as a house painter. The money he made from painting supported his gambling habit at night.

One night, an extremely drunk miner came into the saloon and pulled a knife on Tubbs. Alice quickly whisked out her gun and shot the man in the arm, saving Tubbs's life. Tubbs was impressed by Alice's skill and began to see her in a different light. To him, she was not only a good poker player and a smart woman, she was also beautiful. He fell in love and proposed marriage. Alice said yes.

She did have one stipulation, however. Tubbs would concentrate on his house painting business and she would be the gambler in the family. This plan seemed to work well, and allowed Alice to become the main breadwinner. The couple had seven children through the coming years — four boys and three girls — and Alice kept on playing poker whenever she could. She always said that Tubbs was better at producing children than making a living at gambling, whereas her winnings on any given night could sometimes total as much as $6,000. That kind of money was too hard to resist. As a dealer at the tables, she still attracted any man who was looking for a challenge. Her bland expression while she concentrated on the cards made her the epitome of the "poker-face" player. Even though Alice was gambling to support her family, poker was definitely her calling in life and she most probably would have continued playing anyway. However, while her children were still young, Alice would not allow them anywhere near the gambling halls or ever see their mother at work.

As Alice got older and her children moved away, she and Tubbs retired to a quieter life on a chicken ranch north of Deadwood. But in 1910, his lungs weak from the many years of working with paint, Warren Tubbs contracted pneumonia.

Alice stayed by his side, nursing him through his illness. On one particularly cold and wintry night, he died in Alice's arms. It had been a severe winter, and a blizzard continued to rage for days, but Alice knew it was her husband's wish to be buried back in Sturgis, some 48 miles away. She was determined to carry out his wishes, so she decided to drive his frozen corpse there in a sled, as the snow continued to fall. On arrival, she pawned her wedding ring for $25 to pay for his burial.

After another suitable period of mourning for husband number two, Alice resumed her old profession, taking a table in a gambling hall in Sturgis. Once more, she was doing what she really enjoyed most in life.

Now she took to wearing less glamorous clothing, adopting a khaki skirt, a man's shirt, and an old frayed hat, which, combined with the ever-present cigar hanging from her lip, was how she was always seen in any photograph taken of her.

While Alice gambled in town, she hired a man named George Huckert to tend to her farm. He took an immediate shine to Alice and kept proposing to her. When his back wages totaled over $1,000, Alice agreed to marry him. "It was cheaper to marry him than pay him off," she was quoted as saying. When Huckert proved to be nothing but a loafer who hung out in bars, Alice was almost relieved when he died and made her a widow for the third time. She then decided to take back her previous name of Tubbs.

As the years rolled on, life became tougher for Alice

Ivers Tubbs. Her money had run out and a wave of reform was hitting the gambling halls of Deadwood and Sturgis. Nonetheless, Alice decided to open her own gambling joint in Sturgis. She was betting on the fact that Sturgis was near Fort Meade, where a number of soldiers were stationed. She knew that if she combined gambling with some pretty girls plying their trade for the soldiers from the Fort, she could make a killing.

Alice certainly did well at her new venture. At the same, she began to bootleg alcohol, but once prohibition took effect and more stringent laws were enforced, this became more difficult. Eventually, her business was limited to catering to the soldiers stationed at Fort Meade.

For this, Alice ran afoul of the law and was hauled into jail to face charges of running a house of prostitution and a gambling joint, as well as for possessing liquor. People were still sentimental about Poker Alice, however, and many still loved her brashness and determination. Thus it was that public opinion forced the governor to stay her sentence, and she was set free.

Later, she was charged again, this time with shooting and killing a soldier who was supposedly breaking into her house. She went to jail once more, though she claimed she had shot the man accidentally. As she sat in a cell awaiting a verdict to be brought in by the jury, she read her Bible and prayed. The verdict finally came and she was found not guilty. It was unanimously agreed that the shooting had been in self-defense. When she was well over 70, she was charged on yet another occasion with running a house of prostitution. Alice never gave up and was determined to make money one way or another.

By February of 1930, however, a lifetime of liquor, cigar smoking, and the atmosphere of gambling halls was taking its toll on the once classy lady. Poker Alice began to have gall bladder problems, and her doctors advised an operation. Although it was still a relatively new procedure, Alice decided to take one more gamble and go for the operation. After all, she was only 77, and a fortuneteller had once told her she would live to be 100.

Her last gamble did not pay off. She died on the operating table in a Rapid City Hospital and was buried at St. Aloysius Cemetery in the Black Hills of South Dakota. The history of Poker Alice and her notoriety as a gambler is still told in the annual Deadwood Days festival. She has become one of the most famous of western legends. Her house in Sturgis was saved from demolition by an entrepreneur named Ted Walker, who had it moved to its present location on Junction Avenue, where it is now open daily for tourists.

Her days in all the mining camps of early Colorado are also still celebrated historically throughout the state. Some tales about her daring deeds at the gambling tables have been exaggerated through the years, but most are accurate.

Poker Alice was one of a kind.

Chapter 8

The Dirty Little Coward Who Murdered Mr. Howard

By the mid-1870s, outlaw Jesse James had become a folk hero in the American west. He was adored and admired by many, but perhaps by no one more so than young Bob Ford.

Bob and his older brother, Charlie, were small-time crooks in Missouri. They had both had brushes with the law, but nothing too serious. As a still wet-behind-the-ears teenager, Bob longed to be part of big time crime, whereas Charlie was more content with the status quo.

Bob was born in 1861. His family was average, middle-class, law-abiding folk, but Bob and Charlie were a little different. By the time Bob reached his teens, he had developed a hero worship for Jesse James. The notorious bank and train robber had quite a following of Jesse James wannabes. Bob longed to be just like him, able to pull off amazing heists with ease. He also wanted the same respect that Jesse commanded, but for that he would have needed the charisma that belonged to Jesse James alone.

Like the Ford brothers, Jesse James was born in Missouri on a farm in Kearney, and had a number of brothers, stepbrothers, and stepsisters from his parents' subsequent marriages. He was skilled with horses, but never a particularly good marksman. He had left home in 1863 and joined the infamous Quantrill Raiders, where he first acquired the nickname Dingus. He was involved in many battles and massacres during that time, and at the end of the Civil War was wounded by a bullet that pierced one of his lungs. He was nursed back to health by his cousin Zerelda (Zee) Mimms, who became his friend and, nine years later, his wife.

After the war, Jesse James and his brother Frank joined forces with Cole Younger to form the James-Younger gang, and during the late 1860s and early 1870s, the gang pulled off a number of successful bank and train robberies. Initially, they were not very proficient at the game, but gradually, with Jesse as the mastermind behind most of their operations, the gang became a force to be reckoned with.

During those years, Bob Ford's admiration for Jesse grew. His dream was to become part of Jesse's gang, and even after he heard of the gang's disastrous bank robbery attempt at Northfield, Minnesota, in 1876, he never wavered in his worship of his all-time hero. At Northfield, when the gang rode into town to rob the bank, a number of citizens fought back to protect their money. During the fracas that ensued, some gang members were shot or wounded, while others rode away, pursued by posses. Jesse and Frank James made good their escape but, for the next three years, they lay low, and Jesse took the name of Tom Howard. People reported that the James brothers had lost their nerve after Northfield, but Bob Ford did not believe it. He was sure that his hero was merely biding his time until it was right to strike again, and he was right.

During those three years, Jesse and Zee James (living as Mr. and Mrs. Tom Howard) lived in many parts of the country, moving frequently from one place to another. Zee was happy that her outlaw husband was finally in "retirement." She liked living anonymously as Mrs. Howard because, although she had always known of her husband's activities on the wrong side of the law and had remained faithful to him despite that knowledge, she had always yearned for a more peaceful life. For a while, they settled in California Gulch in Colorado where Jesse worked a rich mine, and that was where Bob Ford finally met up with his hero.

By October of 1879, Jesse and Frank were running short of money. Jesse began recruiting some men who would be trustworthy and would help him form a new gang. He chose gunmen, safecrackers, and others with criminal experience, such as Dick Liddil, Ed Miller, Tucker Basham, and Bill Ryan.

He also picked Bob and Charlie Ford. He trusted Charlie more than he did his younger brother, whom he considered young and inexperienced. He decided, therefore, that he would place Charlie in the middle of the action, but would only give Bob the easy jobs, like being a lookout for the gang.

Bob considered himself as good as the rest, and he vowed he would prove himself to Jesse, one way or another. Meanwhile, Jesse never quite trusted the young, eager boy and always kept a keen eye on him.

Having settled his wife and two children back in Kearney, Jesse and his gang planned their first robbery, which was to hit the Chicago and Alton train at Glendale, Missouri. The job netted them more than $40,000, and Jesse was well pleased. He praised his team, telling them they had played the game well, like old hands, and they should now all lie low for a while. It was not until almost a year later that they robbed a Wells Fargo stagecoach. This job netted a mere $1,400. Subsequent jobs brought them profits of over $5,000 each time. The Jesse James gang was back in action.

The Northfield disaster was now long forgotten, and Jesse's reputation as a larger-than-life, loveable bandit whose adventures thrilled the readers of cheap novels, had been reinstated. During this period, he grew a beard, not just to hide his identity, but also to create the image of the bad guy everyone loved.

Jesse was definitely enjoying himself again, but Bob Ford certainly was not. He still felt like the low man on the totem pole. He yearned for more responsibility and more importance. He did not relish being called "the kid." He had passed 20 by then and felt he deserved more respect.

The gang robbed four more trains in 1881, the last one being in Glendale, Missouri, and each time they made quite a killing. At the same time that Bob was growing restless with his inferior position in Jesse's gang, Missouri's governor, Thomas Crittenden, was becoming extremely concerned about things in general. How long could the state allow these bandits to get away with their outrageous crimes? How long could *he* just sit by and watch while banks and trains and their employees were repeatedly endangered? He decided to offer a large reward — $10,000 — to anyone who would bring in Jesse James, dead or alive! This was the largest bounty placed on anyone's head in American history to that point. Crittenden felt certain the reward would have the desired effect.

And so it was, that as Crittenden lounged in his office on one late afternoon mulling over the situation, his secretary entered and informed him there was someone to see him on a matter of great urgency. Crittenden was irritated. He disliked being disturbed that late in the day. "Visitations are done for the afternoon, John," he replied, continuing to gaze out the window at the rooftops of Jefferson City.

"But, sir, he says this concerns Jesse James the outlaw. He claims he can help us capture him."

Crittenden immediately sat up straight and turned from the window. "Send him in at once!" he said.

The Dirty Little Coward Who Murdered Mr. Howard

The secretary immediately ushered in a young man, and the governor put out his hand. "Hello, son. I'm Governor Tom Crittenden. And you are...?"

"Ford, sir," the young man replied. "My name is Robert Ford."

The two men talked for well over an hour, by which time the office had grown dark, and the sun had long since disappeared beyond the horizon.

Jesse knew there was a large bounty on his head so, for safety's sake, he decided to move his wife and two children out of Kearney, where he figured many bounty hunters might be looking for him. He moved them to a small whitewashed house on a hill overlooking the town of St. Joseph, Missouri, which he rented from a city councilman for $14 a month. He and his family began to attend church, and Jesse resumed his quiet life as Tom Howard. His gang had all gone their separate ways, and his brother Frank was now living with his wife in Tennessee. Only two members of the gang stuck around, Charlie and Bob Ford.

During the winter of 1882, Jesse tried to buy a small farm in Nebraska, but he was just short of the necessary cash. He began to consider ways of finding the money. Meanwhile, both he and Zee had been good to the Ford brothers and even allowed them to stay in their home on occasion. Jesse was beginning to trust Bob more now, so he talked to the Fords about another bank job he was planning at the Platte County Bank. Bob listened attentively.

113

On the morning of April 3, 1882, Jesse was in the parlor with the two brothers, as Zee cooked them all breakfast in the kitchen and the children played in the garden. They were discussing, in whispered tones so that Zee wouldn't hear, the layout of the bank they planned to rob. Jesse figured this one would be easy to take with only three men. He turned to Bob and said, "With the others all gone, we need you, Bob. I think you've been with us long enough to charge the bank."

Bob smiled, but inside he was still feeling angry. Too little, too late, his heart told him — $10,000 in reward money was just too tempting to ignore. Being an informant about the bank robbery was one thing, but this opportunity was even better. He eyed Jesse's gun belt with its Colt guns protruding from each holster. The guns had been set on a highboy, well out of reach of the children, should they come into the room. Jesse was unarmed. Bob's opportunity had come. He began to talk quickly, asking Jesse numerous questions in order to cover up his excitement. Charlie noticed Bob eyeing the guns, and his face grew pale.

Suddenly, Jesse interrupted Bob. "Sorry, Bob, excuse me just a second."

He stood up and tilted his head to one side as he looked at a picture on the wall. "That picture's crooked again. Isn't that the darnedest thing!" He picked up a low stool from the corner and placed it under a small, framed, embroidered picture on the wall, which was slightly crooked.

Jesse was unarmed and preoccupied *and* he had his

back to Bob. With one quick glance at Charlie, Bob jumped up from his chair, pulled out his own pistol from under his coat and fired. Jesse, a mere four feet away, jerked as he grabbed his neck where the bullet penetrated. Bob knew that Jesse had to die. It was too late now to stop what he had started, so he fired three more times to make sure. Half-glancing over his shoulder, an expression of horror on his face, Jesse fell to his death.

Zee immediately ran into the parlor as the two Ford brothers rushed past her and took off through the front door. She saw her husband lying on the carpet beside a pool of blood. In one hand he was still holding the framed piece of embroidery that read: "Bless This House."

The Ford brothers immediately headed to the authorities to claim their reward. Jesse James was dead, they stated, and his body could be found in the Howards's family home at 1318 Lafayette Street in St. Joseph. Much to their chagrin, the Fords were both charged with murder and a trial began, at which they were sentenced to hang. However, because of Bob Ford's earlier conversation with the governor, telling him of his plan, Governor Tom Crittenden pardoned both men. He did not, however, agree to give them the reward money. The plan had just been for Bob Ford to inform the governor of Jesse's next robbery, not to kill him outright.

To make matters worse, Bob and Charlie Ford were labeled cowards. Bob had shot a legend and a hero, and not just in a fair fight, people claimed. Jesse had been shot in the back. The Fords decided it would be safer to leave town.

Bob went first to New Mexico, and then on to Walsenberg, Colorado, where he opened up a saloon and gambling den. Always getting involved in shootings in which he was usually the aggressor, Bob was soon known as a "desperado." He also became an alcoholic, and whenever he got drunk he shot up the town. When he was sober, however, he was peaceful. Something was eating away at him. He boasted continuously that he had slain the great Jesse James single-handedly and had rid the country of the most notorious outlaw America had ever known. He thrived on the attention he received, but deep down he was not a happy man. Sometimes, he charged admission at his saloon to "come and see a re-enactment of the shooting of Jesse James." Some came, but most people were not impressed. After all, Bob Ford had shot their hero. A ballad written about him began with, "Oh, the dirty little coward who shot Mister Howard, and laid Jesse James in his grave. . ."

Bob's brother, Charlie, was not doing well, either. He was finding it even harder to accept being party to what his brother had done. Unable to bear the stigma of being involved in Jesse James' murder, Charlie committed suicide in Richmond, Virginia, a few months later.

When Bob Ford heard about his brother's suicide, he packed up his saloon and gambling equipment in Walsenburg and headed to Creede, where he could make money quickly and be a part of the silver mining rush. He was still a troubled man himself, always looking over his shoulder. In every saloon he visited, he would sit facing the door with a drawn revolver on the table at the ready. He instinctively knew that one day someone would kill him to avenge the killing of Jesse James.

Despite his fears, he settled in Creede and was soon running the Ford Exchange, a prosperous saloon and gambling hall on San Luis Avenue opposite the Fortini Hotel. His Exchange was packed every night, partly because people came to see the man who had shot Jesse James, but mostly because when Ford was sober, he was a good businessman who ran an honest business. Before long, he was considered the top businessman and leader in Creede, employing many people, including Poker Alice, at his tables. He was only challenged for his position as leading citizen on one occasion, when Soapy Smith came to town, but the two men managed to work out an amicable agreement, which enabled both of them to work and make money.

When Bob Ford was drunk, however, he was a different person. On one occasion, after he had placed a large bet on a prize fighter who lost, he went on a drunken spree and threatened to kill the fighter. Then, with a friend in tow, he started shooting out lights in the street and vandalizing property. The citizens of Creede decided that they had finally had enough. Even though this was a lively mining town, Ford was acting wildly and causing too many problems. Vigilantes ordered him out of town by 4 p.m. the following day, on penalty of losing his life.

Ford decided it would be a whole lot better for his health if he complied, so he left for Pueblo by train the very next day. One of the first people he met there was a man named Ed Kelly, and it was a meeting that would later prove fatal. Because of lack of available accommodation in Pueblo, Ford and Kelly were forced to share a hotel room for a while.

Bob Ford began to write letters back to Creede to try and get permission to return. He wrote to all the leading businessmen and stated he would mend his ways and become a respectable citizen. He apologized to the editor of the local paper, asking if he might return, so that he could again run his business there. His letters were not answered. To make matters worse, he awoke one morning to find that Ed Kelly had left; Bob's diamond ring was missing. People later reported that Ed and Bob had also quarreled over a woman. In any event, whatever the truth of the matter actually was, ill feeling had developed between the two men.

Eventually, Bob Ford received word from friends back in Creede that he was going to be allowed to return to run his saloon, as long as he behaved. Bob was delighted and immediately took off, leaving the bad memories of Pueblo behind. What he didn't know was that Ed Kelly was also on his way to the Silver City with a score to settle with him, and it did not just involve a woman or the fact that he was being accused of stealing a ring.

Bob went back to the Exchange, his gambling house in Creede, and began work. His first day back, Kelly entered through the swing doors. Ford immediately went up to him and relieved him of his knife and his gun. "We allow no arms in here, Ed," he said, and then promptly hit Ed over the head with his own pistol. Kelly was incensed. He left, vowing revenge on Bob Ford on many counts. However, on Sunday, June 5, 1892, a fire swept through the town, burning everything in its path, including Ford's Exchange. Bob, like many others in town, was devastated, but he wasted no time and was determined not to allow the disaster to ruin him. He secured some land near a school and erected a tent, announcing it would open the next day, June 8, as a dance hall.

On the afternoon of opening day, Ed Kelly was seen standing outside Bob Ford's temporary dance hall when an unknown cowboy rode by. As he passed, he handed Kelly a double-barreled shotgun. Bob was inside the tent setting things up when Kelly strode in. "Hello there, Bob," he called out. Before Bob Ford could turn, Kelly raised the shotgun and fired both barrels. Ford fell to the ground and died instantly from a wound to the neck, almost exactly where he had shot Jesse James 10 years earlier. Kelly stepped over the body and removed Ford's revolver; then, with the revolver in one hand and the shotgun in the other, he left the tent and gave himself up to Deputy Sheriff Dick Plunkett.

A coroner's jury was summoned, and the court proceedings took place in the dance hall. It was decided that Kelly should be held over for trial, and the deputy from Hinsdale County took over, placing Kelly in a vacant building, where he was closely guarded; officers feared a lynching. The accomplice who had handed Kelly the shotgun was later found. He turned out to be Joe Duvalla, the law officer assigned to guard Kelly. Duvalla subsequently disappeared, no doubt according to plan.

While Kelly was being removed to Lake City for trial, Bob Ford's burial was taking place in Creede. The preacher was unable to think of anything to say about Ford, other than to place him in the hands of his Maker, adding "charity covereth a multitude of sins."

Kelly's case came up on July 7 before Judge John C. Bell, and when the judge asked him how he pleaded, Kelly replied, "Not guilty. I don't rob and I don't insult women, but I kill rats like Bob Ford."

The jury took only 60 minutes to deliberate before finding Ed Kelly guilty of second degree murder. He was given a jail sentence. Before long, however, hundreds of letters began to pour in, all postmarked from Missouri, all seeking clemency for the man who had killed the man who had killed their hero, Jesse James.

Bob Ford's hero worship of Jesse James had turned to anger, greed, and murderous rage, and ultimately gave him nothing but 10 years of dread anticipation, as he waited for the inevitable — his own death at the hand of someone seeking revenge for Jesse's murder.

Ironically, for years there were rumors that perhaps Ford had not been the one who killed Jesse James and that he had simply lied, imagining he would be thought of as a hero. Reports said that James was still alive and well in Oklahoma as late as 1948 and that he eventually died in Granbury, Texas. The man who Ford had killed was supposedly an outlaw named Bigelow, who was living with Jesse's wife at that time.

These statements, however, appear to have been nothing more than straws in the wind. Whatever the truth about the killing of Jesse James, it seemed that Bob Ford did not have one moment of peace in his remaining 10 years on earth. He was young and inexperienced, and the so-called fame he received as James's killer certainly went to his head. He constantly watched his back, expecting that one day someone would get him the same way he had got Jesse James.

For Bob Ford was certainly the real killer. The only question remaining is: was he merely following the governor's orders, or was he really the "dirty little coward" he was purported to be? Only Bob Ford himself knew the truth, and he took that secret with him to his grave.

He is buried in Richmond Cemetery in Missouri, but his headstone bears an incorrect date of birth. It states he was born in 1841 when his real birth was in 1861. Even in death, Bob Ford is still a mystery.

Chapter 9
The Peacekeeper

illiam Barclay Masterson spent only 10 years of his life in Colorado, but the state still proudly claims him as a large part of its history. He is equally well known in Dodge City, Kansas, mainly because of his connection, both as friend and fellow lawman, to Wyatt Earp.

But there was so much more to Masterson. His long and varied career covered many different occupations in many different states. He was a buffalo hunter, an army scout, a gunfighter, a writer, and sports editor, in addition to being one of the most famous lawmen in the west. He loved adventure and he loved life, and his quiet but powerful demeanor gave the State of Colorado confidence during the years he lived there, and earned him the title of "peacemaker." His mere presence on the scene of a dispute, which would otherwise have led to a bloody gunfight, always enabled the matter to be settled calmly and peacefully.

Some references claim he was born in Illinois in 1855, but William Bartholomew Masterson was actually born on November 26, 1853, on a farm near Henryville in Quebec, Canada. His parents, Thomas and Catharine (McGurk) Masterson, had seven children in all; he was their second. The Bartholomew part of his name soon became shortened to Bart or Bat, and it was the name Bat that stuck with him throughout his life.

In 1861, Masterson's family moved to New York State, then to Illinois, and eventually settled in Sedgwick County, Kansas. As a young man, he adopted the name William Barclay (or W. B.) Masterson, which he used for his official signature, but the nickname Bat remained. As a boy, he was never one to enjoy school or book learning. He and his older brother, Ed, much preferred to head off for a day of hunting or fishing, when they should have been in school studying.

In late 1871, having just turned 16, Bat and Ed left the family homestead in search of adventure. The two brothers first worked as graders on the railroad bed for the Atchison, Topeka, & Santa Fe railroad. They then headed to Dodge City, Kansas, where Bat became a buffalo hide hunter and earned a reputation as a crack shot. In the spring of 1874, he accompanied A. C. Myers and Fred Leonard to the Texas Panhandle to help construct the Adobe Walls trading post. Again, he worked as a buffalo hunter in order to supply meat to the railroad crews.

On June 27, 1874, however, a party of Indians, led by Comanche War Chief Quanah Parker, attacked the post just as Masterson and his friend, Billy Dixon, were about to head out on a hunt. As they looked up, they saw the horizon covered with Comanche and Cheyenne warriors. The ensuing battle, which lasted more than six days, cost the lives of four white men and 30 Indians. After it was over, Masterson and Dixon signed on as civilian scouts for the army under Colonel Nelson A. Miles, who had been most impressed with their work during the siege. Masterson's enlistment only lasted until October. He decided he preferred working as a teamster, hauling in supplies to the troops. In the spring of 1875, he was back hunting buffalo and selling their hides in a new town called Sweetwater (later Mobeetie), near Fort Elliott. He was badly wounded in a fight with Melvin King over a woman named Mollie Brennan, and the incident changed the course of Bat Masterson's life.

Masterson, apparently, had asked Mollie to dance, but she was King's girlfriend, and King was a very possessive man. A fight ensued in which Masterson was shot in the leg and Mollie was killed. Masterson retaliated by shooting and killing King, the first and, many believe, the only man he ever killed. Even though it happened in self-defense, he vowed he would never kill again. The fractured bone in his leg caused him to limp for the rest of his life and walk with a cane. After he recuperated, he headed back to Dodge City, where another brother, George, was a bartender at the dance hall and gambling palace known as Varieties. Brother Ed was serving as a deputy under Marshal Wyatt Earp. Knowing Bat's reputation as an honest man, Earp asked him to join his team of law enforcers.

In late 1877, Bat Masterson was elected sheriff of Ford County. The following year, he single-handedly tracked down and apprehended nearly all of the infamous Rourke-Rudabaugh gang, who had been robbing trains at Kinsley, Kansas. He also led the posse that captured the infamous Jim Kennedy, the murderer of well known stage star of the day, Dora Hand.

Then a tragedy occurred back in Dodge, from which Masterson never fully recovered. In April of 1878, his older brother, Ed, was killed in a shoot-out with two outlaws. Bat was so incensed by his brother's murder that he enforced his no gunplay laws and imposed a 9 p.m. curfew in Dodge. He also hired his brother, Jim, as a deputy. In early January 1879, Masterson escorted Henry Born from Colorado back to Dodge to be tried for horse stealing, a serious crime in those days. His impressive record as a law officer led to him being commissioned as a deputy United States marshal that same month.

Masterson still had a strong following in Dodge City, and so he bought an interest in the Lone Star Dance Hall to establish himself as an upstanding citizen and property owner. However, when the elections of 1879 were held there,

Masterson was defeated in his bid for the position of sheriff. Many felt he was too close to the town administrators, especially the mayor, who were all opposed by the reformers in town. Others pointed to the fact that Masterson had spent too much money on the inconclusive trial of seven Cheyenne prisoners he had captured the previous fall.

Soon afterwards, Masterson left for Leadville, Colorado, and spent most of the next 10 years in Colorado, working the gambling tables, drinking and, on occasion, wearing a lawman's badge. From 1880 onwards, he considered Denver his hometown, where he met Emma Walters, a young dancer in the Palace Theatre burlesque troupe. Eventually the two were married. Shortly after the wedding, the couple moved to Creede, where again Masterson managed a saloon and gambling parlor, wore a badge for a while, and served as marshal. He assisted his friend Wyatt Earp on matters of the law and spent time as a sheriff in Las Animas.

Masterson also loved to promote prize fighters, such as John L. Sullivan and Jim Corbett, and he even attended the controversial boxing match in 1896 between Bob Fitzsimmons and Peter Maher, staged by Judge Roy Bean near Langtry, Texas. Prize-fighting had become illegal in most western states by the 1890s, but Roy Bean got around the law by building a bridge to a sandbar on the Rio Grande River and staging this particular fight there, on no man's land. Fitzsimmons decked Maher in 95 seconds, while lawmen looked on from a nearby bluff, unable to do anything. The whole event turned Judge Roy Bean into a legend and gave Bat Masterson an amusing taste of Texan life.

He returned to life in Colorado where, back in 1883, he had been instrumental in persuading the governor to prevent the extradition of Doc Holliday to Arizona, and in 1885 had made a brief stab at the newspaper business by publishing the *Vox Populi*. Unfortunately, the paper folded after only one edition. The following year, he even briefly became a prohibitionist and attempted to close down saloons throughout Colorado and Kansas. Masterson's conversion to a sober life was short-lived, and soon he was back to his old drinking lifestyle in Denver.

It is interesting to note how all these characters of the old west, on both sides of the law, frequently crossed paths. Many of them also spent much of their time drinking and gambling, and Bat Masterson was no exception. His drinking habit worsened by the late 1890s, when he began to associate with gamblers whose reputations were less than respectable. Then, a man named Otto Floto, who owned a rival saloon to Masterson's, began a slanderous attack against Masterson, which culminated in a fist fight on the street. Later Masterson decided to sell out his interest in the club that he owned and, in 1902, public opinion finally forced him and his wife to leave Denver for good.

Perhaps this came as a wake-up call for Masterson. In any event, he decided to move to New York City. Even though the memories of his gun fighting, gambling days throughout

Colorado and Kansas still continued to plague him, he was soon offered a job as deputy United States marshal for the Southern District of New York. The offer came from President Theodore Roosevelt, himself. When Roosevelt left office, President Taft decided he had no further use for Bat Masterson, so Masterson was fired from that position in 1909.

This didn't bother Masterson too much because his friendship with Roosevelt remained intact and, by then, he had also met well-known writer, Alfred Lewis, who later wrote a book about Masterson's life entitled, *The Sunset Trail.* Lewis also encouraged Masterson to go back to his writing and persuaded him to write a series of columns for *Human Life* magazine, telling of his gunfighter days and the people he had met during his life, including stories of his friendships with Wyatt Earp and Doc Holliday.

For Bat Masterson, writing these stories and covering sports events of the era sparked a nostalgic trip back to Dodge City with Alfred Lewis in 1910 to write about the Jack Johnson-Jim Jeffries heavyweight title fight. It became a trip down memory lane for Masterson, and not all the memories were happy ones. His trip took him over the Sante Fe line, on which he had traveled so often in his youth. He passed the fields and plains that had once thundered with the hooves of buffalo. He was pleased to see the changes in Kansas, especially in Dodge, which, he wrote, was "now a thriving little country village, surrounded by a thrifty farming community. There are many of the old-timers still living there and it is doubtful they would care to live elsewhere. They are well-to-do and happy."

Nonetheless, Masterson stood for a moment at a spot on the sidewalk where a now run-down building had once housed the Lady Gay Saloon. It was the exact place where his brother Ed had met an untimely death. Masterson was not one to dwell in the past, though, and his stories of that trip spoke only of the good things that had happened in the city to which he had once tried to bring some semblance of law and order.

His articles continued to flow as he reminisced about his days on the frontier, and throughout them all there was a theme — the necessary qualities needed to be a good lawman. His writings also talked about buffalo hunting, scouting, and some of the gunfights in which he had been involved, especially the one in 1881 when he had returned to Dodge City to help out his younger brother Jim, Dodge's marshal at the time.

Jim also owned a dance hall with his partner, A. J. Peacock. The man they employed as bartender, Al Updegraph, was causing problems for them. Bat arrived in town by train at noon on April 16 that year, and before long, Updegraph challenged him to a gunfight. However, someone else shot Updegraph from behind, the bullet reportedly having come from inside a nearby saloon. Masterson, however, was fined $8 for shooting a pistol in the street.

"I then rode the evening train out of town and vowed that that would be my last gunfight," he wrote. "I was

27 years old at the time."

A man named Frank Ufer, however, obviously jealous of Masterson's successful writing career, started spreading rumors that he had gained his reputation by shooting Mexicans and Indians in the back. Masterson took Ufer to court for his slanderous remarks, and when the matter came before the judge, many scouts, sheriffs, gunfighters, and even the army all testified on Bat Masterson's behalf. He won his case and was awarded $3,000 in damages.

His writings in New York became so popular that eventually he was offered the position of sports editor of the New York *Morning Telegraph*. This he particularly enjoyed because of his love of sport, especially boxing. Masterson also dabbled a little in the political arena and remained a close friend of Roosevelt. It was believed that Masterson was even invited by Roosevelt to discuss military strategy for the Great War. When Roosevelt passed away on January 6, 1919, Masterson was broken-hearted over the loss of his friend.

On the morning of October 25, 1921, Bat sat behind his desk at the *Morning Telegraph*, working on his latest column, and had just written these words:

There are those who argue that everything breaks even, in this dump of a world of ours. I suppose these ginks who argue that way hold that, because the rich man gets ice in the summer and the poor man gets it in the winter, things are breaking even

*for both. Maybe so, but I'll swear that I can't see it
that way ...*

Those were Bat Masterson's last words on this earth.
He collapsed at his desk a few moments later of a heart
attack. His wife died 11 years later in 1932. They had never
had children.

Somehow it seemed that, with the death of Bat
Masterson, the magic of the old west had finally come to
an end.

Epilogue

In 1861, a bill was passed that created Colorado Territory. William Gilpin was appointed by President Lincoln as the state's first territorial governor over a population of approximately 21,000. It was not until 1876 that Colorado was finally admitted as the 38th state in the union and was dubbed the "Centennial State," in honor of the 100th anniversary of the Declaration of Independence.

Following the discovery of gold in California in 1849, other regions, including the Rocky Mountains, were spurred on to find that elusive motherlode. In Colorado, names such as Chicago Creek, Pike's Peak, California Gulch (later Leadville) and Creede all became synonymous with gold or silver towns, which grew at an amazing rate.

And with those towns came the gamblers, the gunmen, and the good-time gals, to spur our imaginations and whet our appetites to know more about the glory of the old wild west.

All of the foregoing stories were about real people. From cannibals to con men, and from gamblers to high-class madams, Colorado's colorful past contained them all.

Further Reading

Burke, John. *The Legend of Baby Doe — The Life and Times of the Silver Queen of the West*. Lincoln: University of Nebraska, 1989 (reprint).

Churchill, E. Richard. *Doc Holliday, Bat Masterson and Wyatt Earp - Their Colorado Careers*. Leadville: Timberline, 1974.

Furman, Evelyn E. Livingston. *Silver Dollar Tabor: The Leaf in the Storm*. Aurora: National Writers, 1982.

Furman, Evelyn E. Livingston. *My Search for Augusta Pierce Tabor, Leadville's First Lady*. Denver: Quality, 1993.

Furman, Evelyn E. Livingston. *The Tabor Opera House — A Captivating History*. Leadville: Leadville Press, 1972.

Jessen, Kenneth, Colorado Gunsmoke: *True Stories of Outlaws and Lawmen on the Colorado Frontier*. Boulder: Pruett, 1986.

Secrest, Clark, *Hell's Belles: prostitution, vice and crime in early Denver*. Boulder: University of Colorado, 2002.

Sprague, Marshall, *Colorado: A Bicentennial History*. New York: Norton, 1976.

Acknowledgments

It has been an incredible pleasure to write about Colorado's historical characters. I first visited Colorado in the 1960s, and it has been most enjoyable to revisit this beautiful state through the stories of these fascinating people. My memories from the 1960s that were growing dim have been delightfully resurrected.

My thanks go to all those who have written about the state in the past, allowing me to research and delve into the lives of these people. I offer my particular thanks to the Colorado State Archives, the Colorado Historical Society, the Denver Public Library, and the Canon City Public Library, for access to materials. And many thanks to the efficiency of the staff at the web site www.askcolorado.com who answered questions so promptly.

I would also like to thank my friends at the Club 44 table — you know who you are — for encouraging me and being so supportive of my writing for more years than I care to remember!

And thank you, David, for understanding that life can become hectic and that housework doesn't always get done when I have three books published in one year!

Acknowlegments

Quotes used in the book were taken from the following web sites:

Confessions of Alfred Packer, Colorado State Archives:
www.colorado.gov/dpa.archives

Colorado History Video Series:
www.leadville.com

Legends of America:
www.legendsofamerica.com

Linda Wommack, *Queens of Market Street:*
www.readthewest.com/wommack

Rocky Mountain News, *Boy Killer Made Colorado History*
Early Settlers from Suffolk:
www.stedmundsbury.gov.uk/earlysettlers

The History of Creede:
www.museumtrail.org/historyofcreede.asp

Photo Credits

About the Author

Valerie Green was born and educated in England, but has lived in Victoria, British Columbia, since 1968, where she actively pursues a career as a freelance writer, columnist, and author of many historical books set in the Pacific Northwest. This is her second book in the *Amazing Stories* series; her first was *Legends, Liars and Lawbreakers: Incredible Tales from the Pacific Northwest.* Her other books have covered many aspects of early life in British Columbia in general and Victoria in particular, a city she moved to in the 1960s for "one year." One husband, two children, and 36 years later, she is still proud to call Victoria home.

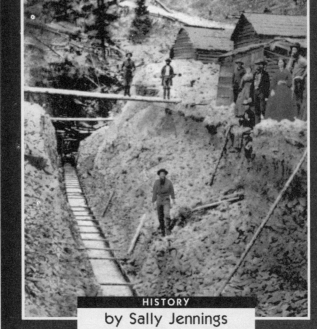

AMAZING STORIES™

COLORADO GHOST TOWN STORIES

Faded Fortunes and Abandoned Dreams

HISTORY
by Sally Jennings

COLORADO GHOST TOWN STORIES
Faded Fortunes and Abandoned Dreams

"I've got all of California right here in my pan!"
Abe Lee on finding gold near Leadville

Eureka! In 1859 gold was discovered in Colorado, sparking a westward rush of thousands of hopefuls in search of riches. Their slogan was "Pikes Peak or Bust." Some miners were lucky. Many were not. This fascinating collection includes many exciting and heartbreaking tales from the gold fields.

True stories. Truly amazing.

ISBN 1-55265-200-9

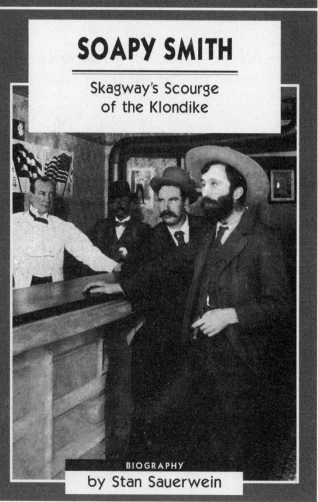

AMAZING STORIES™

SOAPY SMITH

Skagway's Scourge
of the Klondike

BIOGRAPHY
by Stan Sauerwein

SOAPY SMITH
Skagway's Scourge of the Klondike

"Soapy's gang, in the guise of freight agents, newspaper reporters, knowledgeable old-timers, and clergymen, ringed the docks waiting for suckers to arrive."

In 1897, the Klondike Gold Rush brought thousands of hopeful prospectors to the North. With them came many scoundrels and swindlers who were willing to do whatever it took to separate unsuspecting targets from their hard-earned cash. No swindler was more successful at his craft than Jefferson Randolph "Soapy" Smith, who ruled Skagway, Alaska, with a quick hand and a scheming mind. This book explores his most outrageous escapades.

True stories. Truly amazing.

ISBN 1-55439-011-7

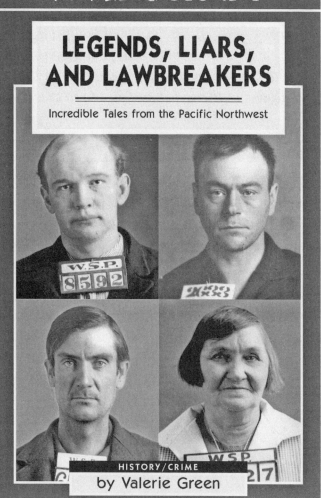

AMAZING STORIES™

LEGENDS, LIARS, AND LAWBREAKERS

Incredible Tales from the Pacific Northwest

HISTORY/CRIME

by Valerie Green

LEGENDS, LIARS, AND LAWBREAKERS

Incredible Tales from the Pacific Northwest

"I hate Sin. You know that. But I love Sinners."
Reverend Dr. Mark Matthews

Throughout history some people have pushed the limit of what is acceptable to society. Those featured in this book lived in an era when smuggling was rife, liquor was plentiful, and murder was rampant. Many become legends in their own lifetimes and, although often feared and loathed, are remembered as colorful characters who were products of the times in which they lived.

True stories. Truly amazing.

ISBN 1-55153-771-0